With a pastor's touch, and a
Milton's new volume offers
to one of life's most importar
I am called to the ministry?' ___ ~~~~~~~-soaked wisdom
offered here will help put godly pastors in the pulpits—
something we need now more than ever.

Michael J. Kruger

President and Samuel C. Patterson Professor of New
Testament and Early Christianity, Reformed Theological
Seminary

I have known Pastor, Professor and President Mike Milton
for many years. I love him; I love his love for ministry, and
I love reading of how the Lord has guided Mike's calling
so that he may share his love with others so called.

Bryan Chapell

Pastor, Grace Presbyterian Church, Illinois

Dr. Milton is supremely qualified to give advice on the
pastoral call to ministry. When asked for advice as to how
to discern a call to ministry (a question I am often asked),
I will now say with confidence, 'You should read Mike
Milton's book. It will answer most if not all of your questions.' This new book is a marvellous resource which I
look forward to seeing very soon.

Derek W. H. Thomas

Senior Minister, First Presbyterian Church, Columbia,
Chancellor's Professor, Reformed Theological Seminary
Teaching Fellow, Ligonier Ministries

Seminary students need discipling, coaching, and mentoring from experienced pastors who can help them understand their call to ministry. My friend and colleague, Mike Milton, draws on his vast experience as church planter, pastor, chaplain, theologian, and leader extraordinaire to offer wisdom to our young Timothies. This book is a treasure and I recommend it for seminarians and seasoned ministers alike.

R. J. Gore Jr.
Professor of Systematic Theology and Ministry;
Dean, Erskine Theological Seminary;
Retired Chaplain (COL) USA

CALLED?

PASTORAL GUIDANCE
FOR THE DIVINE CALL
TO GOSPEL MINISTRY

MICHAEL A. MILTON

CHRISTIAN
FOCUS

CALLED?

paperback ISBN 978-1-5271-0112-8
epub ISBN 978-1-5271-0194-4
mobi ISBN 978-1-5271-0195-1

Published in 2018
by
Christian Focus Publications Ltd,
Geanies House, Fearn, Ross-shire
IV20 1TW, Scotland
www.christianfocus.com

Cover design by Pete Barnsley

Printed and bound by Bell & Bain

MIX
Paper from
responsible sources
FSC
www.fsc.org
FSC® C007785

CONTENTS

The Reverend Michael A. Milton, MPA, PhD (University of North Carolina at Chapel Hill; University of Wales) is a Presbyterian minister, author, composer, United States Army Chaplain (Colonel), and presently serves as the James H. Ragsdale Chair of Missions and Evangelism at Erskine Theological Seminary in South Carolina. He is also the President of Faith for Living at the D. James Kennedy Institute for Reformed Leadership. A singer-songwriter with five albums released, he was senior minister of the historic First Presbyterian Church of Chattanooga.

Milton also founded two other congregations (Kansas and Georgia) and is presently founding pastor of Trinity Chapel Charlotte (ARPC) in Weddington, North Carolina. Milton is a graduate of MidAmerica Nazarene University (BA), Knox Theological Seminary (MDiv), University of North Carolina at Chapel Hill (MPA), and University of Wales (PhD). Both descendants of the founding families of Virginia and North Carolina, Mike and Mae Milton reside in the Charlotte area. They are avid gardeners of hybrid roses.

For the glory of Almighty God:
Father, Son, and Holy Spirit;
and for my wife, Mae.

Acknowledgments

Paul gives this teaching to Christians, persons who knew themselves 'called,' to assure them of present security and final salvation, and to make them realize the extent of their debt to God's mercy, and so lead them into great gratitude for great grace—David L. Jeffrey.[1]

A reworking and updating of an earlier work is no less time-consuming than the original. Indeed, in many ways, it requires double-effort! We had to not only edit the first copy, but also, add updated material that we wished we had included. Additionally, we trust this book can stand on its own as a contribution to the larger field of pastoral theology. In that effort, I am most appreciative to those who helped me make this project a reality.

Firstly, let me say thank you to the Christian Focus staff. I have been a partner with them in seeking to disseminate

---

1   *A Dictionary of Biblical Tradition in English Literature* (Grand Rapids, MI: W.B. Eerdmans, 1992).

Biblical and evangelical literature through the years. It is always a great honor and privilege to work with them. Thank you.

As I write, I have re-entered the shepherding life of a working pastor. Trinity Chapel Charlotte is a Presbyterian Church (ARPC) in the Weddington, North Carolina community just south of Charlotte. My executive assistant, Mrs. Christine Hartung, has been an indispensable and cheerful assistant in my pastoral work for some time now. I am deeply appreciative to her for her constancy and wisdom in all things administrative. To Rev. William 'Tripp' Castell III, Professor Don Piers II, and to the emerging congregation of that church: I thank you. The Provisional Session of Trinity Chapel Charlotte forms a wise and anointed spiritual covering for this fledgling new work. Thanks to my colleagues, Rev. Mike Jones, at Outreach North America, and Rev. Morrie Lawing at First Presbytery. I am always grateful to Mrs. Nancy Tuberville, pastor's wife and a friend to my own wife. Thanks Dean and Nancy.

I am very thankful to Erskine Theological Seminary: to the students, fellow faculty members, staff, administration, and board for their support. The board of trustees of that venerable institution recently honored my wife and myself with the invitation to prepare pastors and missionaries for Christian service through the auspices of the Reverend Dr. James H. Ragsdale Chair of Mission and Evangelism. Our hearts have been greatly moved by the ministry there. We are thankful that we can, through this ministry, and the D. James Kennedy Institute for Reformed Leadership, labor to produce materials for the Associate Reformed Presbyterian Church, the Presbyterian and Reformed community of churches in the world, and, most broadly and intentionally, for the *Church catholic* of our God and Savior Jesus Christ. This book and so much other work would be impossible without the support of those mentioned and so many others. Robin Broome, Director of Admissions at Erskine College and Seminary, is due credit, for her many acts of Gospel charity as she supports my academic efforts there.

The pastorate is like a bouquet of flowers. Each congregation, every staff member, and, indeed, each community becomes a unique placement of bright and refreshing flowers in the larger vase of vocation. In my case, I see a bouquet before me of friends, parishioners, fellow ministers, and leaders from New Hope Presbyterian Church in Olathe, Kansas; Coral Ridge Presbyterian Church in Fort Lauderdale, Florida; Redeemer Presbyterian Church in Overland Park, Kansas (along with Heritage Christian Academy); Knox Theological Seminary; Kirk O' the Isles Presbyterian Church in Savannah, Georgia; First Presbyterian Church of Chattanooga; Reformed Theological Seminary; and an interim pastorate at Church of the Redeemer (PCA) in Monroe, North Carolina.

Since several friends suggested a re-working of an earlier work, and wisely guided us to consider amendments that would give attention to Christians in the emerging parts of the world where the Church is growing, we have had the considerable job of editing some very U.S. and North American-centric material. For this I enjoyed the assistance of Dr. Rebecca Rine of Grove City College. Dr. Rine, as with previous projects, proved to be invaluable in helping me discover 'better ways to say it better' and more often to know when to keep quiet. Although I suspect the reader will find some remaining concerns in the former and, no doubt, several occasions of the latter, those occasions will be mine to correct. She did splendid work. Thank you, Rebecca. I must also give public acknowledgement to Dr. Larry Dixon, recently retired professor from Columbia International University. His suggestions and edits proved invaluable in the final stages of this work.

I want to also acknowledge the wisdom of my home church pastor, the Rev. Robert E. Baxter. For almost three decades now he has been a constant source of inspiration and guidance to me throughout all my pastoral ministry. 'Pastor Bob' guided me in the early days as I was struggling with the call and as I write this he is still in pastoral practice himself, providing a faithful model to me and to many others.

I want to mention several others who encouraged this project: the Soldiers, Families, and Civilian employees of the U.S. Army Chaplain School, especially the Commandant, Chaplain (Colonel) Peter Sniffin (and, later, my old friend, Chaplain, Colonel Jeffery D. Hawkins); the Military Intelligence Readiness Command, where I serve as Command Chaplain (I am about to retire); and the Reverend Doug Lee, Chaplain (Brigadier General), Executive Director of the Presbyterian and Reformed Commission on Chaplains.

I have the joy of holding dual credentials with both the Tennessee Valley Presbytery of the Presbyterian Church in America and First Presbytery of the Associate Reformed Presbyterian Church. I pray that I will represent them well and acknowledge the joy of collegiality within these august bodies.

How do I say thank you to my son, John Michael, for our long rides and long talks about culture, pastoral work, calling, creativity, art, worldview, and comic books? This 'call out' cannot begin to do it! But a father's smile might just reveal the depth of my gratitude for your filial honor shown. Thank you.

As usual I wish to thank my wife, Mae, for her devotion to Christ expressed through her loving support of the ordained ministry as we have served in ministry over the years to many others. She is indefatigable in spirit and strong of heart and mind as she demonstrates, daily, not only the model of a pastor's wife, but, quite simply, the life of a disciple. 'But a woman that feareth the LORD, she shall be praised' (Prov. 31:30).

With sincere gratitude to each and every person that I've named and with apologies for those that I simply couldn't include, I must add that necessary, quite obligatory, closing statement in the acknowledgments that all remaining errors are the author's responsibility.

Preface

… And then the justice, In fair round belly with good capon lin'd, With eyes severe, and beard of formal cut, Full of wise saws and modern instances; And so he plays his part—William Shakespeare.[1]

This book is one of the several projects that I am working on at this time, that I would classify according to the above description. One might say that a keeper of meaning seeks to dispatch wisdom in the service of justice. In this book a keeper of meaning in the ministry pursues insight in the service of vocation for the glory of God and the advancement of the Kingdom of Jesus Christ.

I wrote *Leaving a Career to Follow a Call: A Vocational Guide to the Ordained Ministry*[2] in the year 2000. Since then we have seen the need to add to that work and to enlarge its vision (and correct editorial errors). That is the

---

1   *As You Like It.* Act II, Scene vii, 7.

2   Eugene Oregon: Wipf and Stock Publishers.

humble genesis of this book. Our nonprofit organization published *Lord, I Want to Follow Your Call,* another revision, to help seminary students in my classes. Yet it developed from there with prayerful intentions to become a guide to self-study for pastoral ministry for the global Church.

The present volume is intended to serve the Church in her preparation of servants for the holy office of the ordained ministry. We seek to present this work for all of the Church universal. Indeed, we have paid renewed attention to the movement of the Lord in our generation as the Church has grown and expanded greatly in the global South and the global East. We trust that this new work, though certainly building on the earlier effort, will now also reflect our greater concern for the catholicity of the Church, not only in doctrinal expression, but also in geographic representation. Furthermore, we did not wish to perpetuate prior assumptions about academic credentials and ordination. The state of that subject continues to change in Great Britain, Western Europe, the British Commonwealth nations, and North America, but is markedly different in the 'Next Christendom.'[3] While the Master of Divinity and Master of Arts with pastoral internship continues to predominate in the Western nations, there is greater attention being given to how the 'anatomy' of theology and the 'residency' requirements of that spiritual medical school

---

3   I am using the helpful term from Philip Jenkins, *The Next Christendom: The Coming of Global Christianity* (Oxford: Oxford University Press, 2002).

(AKA 'seminary') might be expressed in other ways. The Church in the 'global South' (Jenkins, 2002) and the 'global East' (Jenkins) is now affecting the Western Church.

There have also been remarkable advances in distance learning. Auden wrote that 'We would rather be ruined than changed'[4] and this—it seems to me—applies to many working in the field of theological higher education today. The truth is that synchronous and asynchronous platforms have allowed for high quality delivery of theological education. This has had an enormous impact for the 'medical school' component of pastoral preparation. There is, of course, the 'residency' component, which must remain face-to-face Parish encounter. So, it seems that technology here can be the servant of missions. So, I have tried to adapt some of the things in the book to these recent technological advances which I see as tools to the ministry and 'Roman roads' over which we can travel to bring the gospel of Jesus Christ.

Despite all the changes and the diverse expressions of how the divine call is expressed, the nature of the call remains as it was when Abraham left Ur or when Peter and Andrew left their nets at Galilee. The goal of this book, then, is to reveal that glorious call and to, hopefully, provide a pastoral guide to the passage that may very well be awaiting even the one who now reads these words. If so, may God grant you His Holy Spirit's anointing as you read. May His Word that may be taught aright in this

---

4   W. H. Auden, *The Age of Anxiety: A Baroque Eclogue* (New York: Random House, 1947).

little volume be brought to your mind and heart in good ways, helping you to make your way onward and upward.

M.A. Milton
Matthews, North Carolina, USA
Palm Sunday 2016

1

A Theology of Calling

Following my call was indeed the most wonderful thing I ever did. The mind of man will never comprehend the wonder, the mystery, or the operational ramifications of this miracle we know as 'the call.' But the pages that follow will assuredly add more to the reader's understanding and appreciation of this sacred encounter with the Holy Spirit than before.—Dr. D. James Kennedy (1930-2007)[1]

If you are reading this book, you mostly likely believe—or at least suspect—that God has a 'call' on your life. You are considering what your vocation is and should be.

The Latin *vocare*, from which we get our English word 'vocation,' means to call, to summon. Therefore, when we speak of vocation in this book, we are speaking of one's calling in life.

How can we attune our ears to hear God's call? There are many wonderful books on calling. Edmund Clowney's

---

1   From the Introduction, Michael A. Milton, *Leaving a Career to Follow a Call: A Vocational Guide to the Ordained Ministry* (Eugene, Oregon: Wipf and Stock Publishers, 2000).

Called to the Ministry is among the best.[2] I will not try to cover or even summarize all of the excellent teaching on this subject that you can find elsewhere. But before I delve more deeply into this topic, I do want to briefly review what it means to be 'called' in the biblical sense.

THE BIBLICAL UNDERSTANDING OF CALLING

The Word of God describes several kinds of calling, including a general call to everyone, an effectual call to His people, and what we might describe as a technical call to a particular vocation in life.

God gives the general call to every creature on earth. We are all called to turn away from our sins and to turn toward God and His plan for our salvation. This is the 'fundamental prerequisite for the performance of any Christian service.'[3] We are all called to live according to God's law; we are all called to a life of service to God and our fellow man. So, every Christian—indeed, every person on earth—has a calling of a sort. This is known as God's general call.

Many Christians such as myself believe (along with Calvin and other Reformers) that there is also an effectual calling. In the effectual calling, the Holy Spirit improves

2   See the Reading List at the end of this book. For a scholarly treatment of the minister's call, see *The Southern Presbyterian Review*, No. II, September, 1848, 'The Call to the Ministry—Its Nature and Evidence.'

3   Samuel T. Logan, Jr., ed., 'The Minister's Call' by Joel Nederhood, *The Preacher and Preaching: Reviving the Art in the Twentieth Century* (Phillipsburg, New York: Presbyterian and Reformed Publishing Company, 1986), 45.

upon the general call and makes it lead to salvation. Those who respond to Christ in faith are the recipients of this effectual, internal call.

We may also observe from the Bible a third kind of call, a technical call. This is a calling related to one's life's work. John Calvin wrote,

> *This point is to be noted: the Lord bids each one of us in all life's actions to look to his calling. For He knows with what great restlessness human nature flames, with what fickleness it is borne hither and thither, how its ambition longs to embrace various things at once. Therefore, lest through our stupidity and rashness everything be turned topsy-turvy, He has appointed duties for every man in his particular way of life. And that no one may thoughtlessly transgress his limits, He has named those various kinds of livings 'callings.' Therefore each individual has his own kind of living assigned to him by the Lord as a sort of sentry post, so that he may not heedlessly wander about throughout life.*[4]

Calvin taught that all men and women have a calling in life, and that it is their duty to investigate the gifts and circumstances of their lives to discover and exercise that calling to the glory of God. Of course, this doctrine brought enormous joy to the humble workers of that day, as it should today.

Within that broader technical calling, there are those who are a part of God's kingdom (that is, those who have received an effectual call) who are also called to a certain, peculiar work in the kingdom.

---

4   See *Institutes of the Christian Religion*, John T. McNeil, editor (Philadelphia: The Westminster Press, 1960), pp. 724-725.

For instance, some are called to go and journey to another land (such as Abraham). Others may receive a technical call to do something as special as bearing the Son of God (there's only one of those: Mary!). Others (and this is our concern at present), having been called to repentance and faith, having been summoned by God Himself to be a part of His kingdom, receive a technical call to preach and minister in His name. Among those we would include the prophets and the apostles.

A powerful example of one who knew he had this particular technical call was the Old Testament prophet Amos. Amos had been called by God to leave his humble rural life to journey to the Northern Kingdom of Israel with a divine warning. At Bethel, the capital of the Northern Kingdom, Amaziah the priest got wind of Amos' prophecies. He went to the king, Jeroboam, and conspired to get rid of Amos. 'The land is not able to bear all his words,' he said (Amos 7:10). Amos answered:

> *I was no prophet, nor was I a son of a prophet, But I was a sheep breeder and a tender of sycamore fruit. Then the LORD took me as I followed the flock, and the LORD said to me, 'Go, prophesy to My people Israel.' Now therefore, hear the word of the LORD... (Amos 7:14-16).*

In this passage, Amos grounds his authority to preach to the resistant hearers solely on his technical call. In fact, he tells us here that he once had another technical call—to be a sheepbreeder and tender of sycamore trees—but that now the Lord has commanded him to prophesy.

If you are reading this book, it is likely that you, or someone you know well (perhaps a spouse, a sibling, a child, a parent, or a good friend), is in the process of considering whether or not he or she has a technical call to ministry. Discerning this carefully, and gaining clarity on the nature of the call, is one of the most important things you can be doing right now.

I am reminded of my own experience of discerning my technical call. The significance of this stage of the process was pressed home to me by an aging Nazarene preacher who once asked me, 'Son, are you called?' I said, 'I think so.' He asked again, 'Son, I said, "Are you called?"' He grew somewhat agitated. So did I. I answered once more, 'Yes, I think I am.'

He then drew closer to me and looked me right in the eye. 'Son, you'd better *know* you are called. In the end, your call is all you got. When they spread rumors about you, when they reject you, when they betray you, when they run you out of town, the only thing that will stand you in good stead will be that you know that you know that you know that you are called. Now go home and pray until you know!'

Those were good words. Amos knew. Amos could withstand the pressure of the priest and the king because he knew that he knew that he knew that he was called.

So too must you know that you are called.

CLARIFICATION OF THE CALL INWARD AND OUTWARD

How do we know we are called? Not many of us will receive a blinding light on a road to Damascus like Paul did. Not all of us will be in the field one day and in the pulpit the next and suddenly know that we are called. Most of us will go through a process, a process that takes time and involves the influence and insight of several people.

Again, John Calvin is helpful to all of us when we come to this point. He reminds us that, in order to know the nature of our vocation, we must have an 'inward call' and an 'outward call' working together. In fact, one without the other will invalidate what we might think is a call.

The inward call is that stirring of God in our hearts, in our deepest persons. It is the 'Hound of Heaven' of Francis Thompson's classic poem.[5] It is a:

> *secret call of which each minister is conscious before God, and which does not have the church as witness. But there is the good witness of our heart that we receive the proffered office not with ambition or avarice, not with any other selfish desire, but with a sincere fear of God and desire to build up the church. That is indeed necessary for each one of us if we would have our ministry approved by God.*[6]

The outward call, on the other hand, is the ordinary 'outward and solemn call which has to do with the public order of the church.'[7] It is interesting to note that the outward call sometimes appears at first via the most humble of means. Often, we who are in the ministry can recall a single comment by, say, an elderly lady in the Sunday school class who remarked, 'Son, that was

---

5   See 'The Hound of Heaven' by Francis Thompson, with an Introduction by G.K. Chesterton (Brandon Publishing, 1996).

6   *Institutes*, IV.3.10, pp. 1062-63.

7   Ibid.

wonderful. Have you ever thought about the ministry?' It may happen in another way, but most of us can point to a comment and a situation similar to that, which was a crystallizing event in clarifying our sense of call. In some way, our fittingness for the ministry has been recognized in a public way.

Of course, there is much more to receiving an outward call than simply the encouragement of one or two church members. Most denominations are good at helping candidates clarify this kind of call. On the other hand, it takes a great deal of prayer and earnest soul work in order to clarify the inward call. If you are struggling through that as you read, don't give up! Seek the blessing of the Truth for your own life. You will have heard it said that if you can do something else other than preach, then, do it. But, if after you have considered all, you say with Paul in 1 Corinthians 9:16 '…for necessity is laid upon me; yes, woe is me if I do not preach the gospel!', then come and join this ministry!

2

Reflections on Calling

The ministry had long been the profession of his choice, and was doubtless the only profession which he had ever thought of pursuing.—Jonathan Edwards[1]

It is one thing to be able to describe a theology of calling and to know what to look for when seeking out one's vocation. It is another thing to experience 'being called.'

While every person's situation is different, I have found that one of the best ways to discern calling in my own life is to hear how such a calling has appeared in others' lives. With this in mind, I offer this account of my own experience of being called into full-time ministry. You will see here the pattern of an inward and outward call, as well as the pattern of responding to God's general, effectual, and technical calls.

I am a child of the church. Baptized as an infant at Felicity Methodist Episcopal Church in New Orleans,

---

1   Jonathan Edwards, *The Works of Jonathan Edwards*, vol. 1 (Banner of Truth Trust, 1974), lxxix.

Louisiana, I was subsequently reared at Amite (Southern) Baptist Church in Denham Springs, Louisiana. Following a marked departure from the Lord and the things of God, I pursued a prodigal path that led me, at length, to the harsh awareness that I was eating husks in the hog pen. I did everything wrong and sinful one can do short of getting locked up or falling prey to an addiction.

You can imagine the sordid tales of broken relationships, regrettable decisions, and misery which mark so many lives like mine. But by the grace of God, there came a defining moment in which I realized my sin and began a spiritual quest for home.

During that journey, I became a lay preacher in the United Methodist Church and later in the Episcopal Church, and I then returned to my engagement in the Southern Baptist Church. But for all of my religious interests, and by then, well-seasoned churchmanship, I was still far from the Father's house. It was not until I agreed to go to an Evangelism Explosion (EE) clinic in 1986 that I came to see truly who I was and who God is.

Robert Farrar Capon wrote that every minister must point to a time when he '... developed... a passion for the Passion.'[2] My passion for *the Passion* came via the truths I learned at Evangelism Explosion. I recognized my own sinfulness, God's holiness, and the love, mercy, and grace available in Jesus Christ. I also, for the first time, understood my responsibility to take the Great Commission seriously

2   Robert Farrar Capon, *The Foolishness of Preaching: Proclaiming the Gospel against the Wisdom of the World* (Grand Rapids: Eerdmans, 1998), 8.

and to be obedient to it. Indeed, I like to say that at EE, I received 'spiritual open heart surgery.' I experienced new life in Jesus Christ for the first time and quickly rushed home to tell my wife, Mae. I will never forget the moment that my wife and I knelt beside the sink in our master bathroom and committed our lives to Jesus Christ as our Lord and to being His servants. That was the beginning. I was finally 'home' in my relationship to Jesus Christ—but His work with me was just beginning.

By this time in my professional career, I had been an account manager for two Fortune 500 organizations. Within days of my experience at Evangelism Explosion and our new commitment to Christ, I was greeted by my boss at a hastily called airport meeting in which he announced that I had been promoted to the position of district manager in Kansas City. Soon, with my wife and her daughter, whom I had taken to raise as my own, I was off to the Midwest.

The influence of reading several Reformed authors brought me into contact with the Presbyterian Church in America (PCA), and we immediately sought out and joined a PCA church in Olathe, Kansas. There our family was put in an incubator of sorts under the fine preaching ministry of a godly pastor and in the midst of a loving congregation. We learned what the family could be from our pastor and what the church could be from our fellow parishioners.

During that time I became an adult Sunday school teacher, started Evangelism Explosion at that local church, and served in several other ways as well. My wife taught in the children's ministry, and our daughter was active in the youth group. Soon the people of that church elected me to the office of ruling elder. I was ordained, and upon my ordination began to pour myself, joyfully, into the work of the Presbytery and General Assembly of my denomination. There has never been a greater time of growth for my family.

Sometime during that period, I was disturbed in the inner man, once more, by the pursuit of Thompson's divine Hound. Increasingly, I came to realize a gnawing awareness that God had given me a passion for His Word and for His people—those who were found, and especially in my case, those who were still lost and needed to be reached. In addition to the Hound of Heaven barking inside of me, I began to hear remarks like these:

> *That was a great teaching in our class. You know, Mike, I've been meaning to say this for some time; we think…well, we believe that you should be a minister! Our church needs men like you!*

> *Mike, you and Mae are just meant for the ministry!*

Those comments formed a discernible barking of the Hound of Heaven.

For me, the inner and outer stimuli together were forming an undeniable sense of call to the ministry of Word and Sacrament in the Church.

When I began to hear this call, my first reaction was, 'I am not worthy.' Then, having convinced myself of that, I did what any other honest Jonah would do: I bought a ticket for Tarshish! For me, Tarshish was to be law school.

I had, of course, told my wife about my sense of call. I had told her all of the reasons why I was called, but also assured her that my innate unworthiness would prevent it from going any further. That simple reality, I suggested to her with an air of decisiveness, would keep me from the path toward ministry.

As I proclaimed that I was going to Law School at the University of Kansas, with a tremulous buoyancy, Mae listened. That's it. She just listened! And her silent listening was bearing witness to a God-given female intuition that I recognized. Honestly, I don't think she ever said a word. *I hated it when she did that!* I wanted her to agree with me. I always got the feeling that she knew better than I what the outcome was going to be, yet she was wise enough to wait for me to see it for myself. In any case, with a call and with tickets to the 'Tarshish' Law School in hand, I sought to smother the idea of ordained ministry.

Of course, the story needs go no further at that point. The process only went so far as an application form before I realized that I was dreadfully unhappy and, in fact, on the verge of sin by running from God. My sense of call and responsibility was that real to me, even though I didn't fully understand yet how God would bring His will to pass.

During this period of wrestling with the call, the youth minister at my church suggested I read a book entitled simply *Called to the Ministry,* by Edmund Clowney. That book, perhaps more than any other, helped me to analyze my situation in comparison with others, within the context of Scripture. I felt more strongly than ever that

I was bound with some sort of holy chains to the gospel ministry. But after reading that book, I began to sense that the only way to find freedom was by surrendering to life in the 'chains' of ministry. For the first time I understood Paul's outlook when he wrote, '…woe is me if I do not preach the gospel!' (1 Cor. 9:16).

At this point, I went to speak with my pastor. I told him my story. Though I didn't know these terms at the time, I told him about the inward call and outward call I was experiencing. I told him about my application to law school and my attempt to run from God. I told him how I felt that if I failed to pursue this idea of the ministry to its end, whatever that might be, I would feel like I was sinning. I went into great detail with my own testimony and how I felt that I was not the kind of man God would want as a minister. He listened. Then he spoke.

My pastor confirmed that he had seen God's hand on me and believed that God was calling me to the ministry. It would be a great sacrifice to leave my career as a manager for a Fortune 500 company. It would require the agreement of my wife to make such a transition. Yet my past, he assured me, was similar to that of the apostles and prophets who had been called out of lives of disobedience and sin into the service of the Savior. He saw no reason why I could not begin the long and arduous process of moving to the ordination as a minister of the gospel within our denomination.

The only thing holding me back, then, was my own commitment to leaving my career and following that call.

My pastor agreed to pray with me about my decision and to help me in the process when I told him I was ready.

The grace and peace I found in those few moments in that pastor's study have lasted for over a quarter of a century now. I went home in tears and told my wife about my meeting with the pastor. She told me that she had always known I was called to the ministry. She had seen my agonizing struggle to come to grips with it. It was, though, something that I had to do. She assured me that she would be there and would follow me if I surrendered to the Lord. Her support was the final confirmation of my call.

There would be no turning back.

3
Examples of Calling

The world is charged with the grandeur of God.
It will flame out, like shining from shook foil;
It gathers to a greatness, like the ooze of oil
Crushed. Why do men then now not reck his rod?
Generations have trod, have trod, have trod;
And all is seared with trade; bleared, smeared with toil;
And wears man's smudge and shares man's smell: the soil
Is bare now, nor can foot feel, being shod.
And for all this, nature is never spent;
There lives the dearest freshness deep down things;
And though the last lights off the black West went
Oh, morning, at the brown brink eastward, springs
Because the Holy Ghost over the bent
World broods with warm breast and with ah! bright wings.
—'God's Grandeur' (1877) by Gerard Manley Hopkins
(1844-1889) [1]

The poetry of Gerard Manley Hopkins is not to everyone's liking. I do like this poem and included it as an introduction

---

1   Gerard Manley Hopkins, *'God's Grandeur' and Other Poems* (New York: Dover Publications, 1995).

to the chapter because I like the metaphor of the electrical energy of God building throughout creation, evident in all areas of life. Yet mankind is brought before the bar of God's presence and goodness with a question by this English Catholic writer: 'Why do men then now not *reck* his rod (i.e. heed His word)?' The pressing word here is 'now.' It is time to take notice of God. It is time to follow. Are there any who have? Where are they? Have they left a pathway in the wood for us to follow, too? Indeed, is it ever too late to heed His Word? To *reck His rod? To follow His call?*

As I have talked with potential candidates for ministry over the years, I have noticed that many of them are unsure about the timing of God's call. Those who are very young say, 'But I don't have enough experience yet!' Or, they simply do not consider that God may be calling them to ministry at all. They are much too focused on preparing for a career to consider a 'career' within the church.

On the other hand, those who have already entered a career may wonder if it is too late to receive God's call. 'I have chosen my path already,' they may say, 'and now it is too late for me to change course mid-career.' Often people in this position worry that they are being disobedient to God's call, but they also seem frozen in place, unable to make the shift from their present circumstances to a new environment and priorities.

This chapter will address both those who are young and those who are old, for in the pages of God's Word we see that God calls individuals into the ministry at all phases of life and in very diverse circumstances.

Below, I will first address those who might think themselves 'too old,' and then those who consider themselves 'too young.' Perhaps you will see yourself in both of these.

SECOND CAREER CALLS

Robert N. Rodenmayer, in the Kellogg Lectures at Episcopal Theological School in February of 1958, delivered a series of addresses on the role and work of the modern pastor. In noting how individuals decide to go into the ministry, he had this to say, which is of particular interest to us:

> *There are persons who come into the ministry after years of doing something quite different. A man may have thought seriously of this calling years ago and have given it up for a number of reasons. Then he marries, raises his children, and makes a living. But the old vision persists and he finds himself in seminary years later with the understanding and frequently with the financial support of his wife. Sometimes a mature man with a successful career comes into the ministry because of the insight and perception of his own pastor.... I know of more than one man who in the middle life has begun thinking toward the ministry because some tragic occurrence in his family was met with love and compassion by the local pastor.*[2]

If this was so in 1958, it is even more so today. Yet, strangely, you may hear of those who find the whole matter of leaving a career to follow a call a bit irresponsible.

The truth is that some mistakenly believe that the trend of older seminarians is out of sync with the history

---

2   Robert N. Rodenmayer, *We Have This Ministry* (New York: Harper & Brothers, 1959), 18-19.

of the church. I think there is enough evidence, biblical and historical, to suggest that they are wrong. It is true that a thirty-seven-year-old seminarian was not the norm within American seminaries during the 18th and 19th centuries, but there have always been men who have been called from a prior career to the work of the Lord. In fact, the Bible is replete with such models. We will consider four: Abraham, Moses, the disciples, and Jesus Himself.

ABRAHAM

Genesis 12:1 records the call of Abraham:

Now the LORD had said to Abram: 'Get out of your country, from your family and from your father's house, to a land that I will show you.'

Genesis 12:4 tells us that Abram was seventy-five years old. That is, he was not exactly a college sophomore! God called an older man from a well-settled life and sent him to establish a new nation. In Abraham, God had a man with experience—experience in dealing with people, in managing the affairs of his large household (Gen. 12:5), and in the ebb and flow of day-to-day life. God had waited until Abram was well qualified for the divine task of raising up a new nation before He called him.

Of course, Abram still made mistakes, but they were generally mistakes of character (Genesis 16 and the incident with Hagar; Genesis 20 and his lack of faith and lie about Sarah to Abimelech), and not the mistakes of a man who had never led people. His experiences stood him in good stead, though God still had to sanctify Abram to the work wherein he was called.

God has always called older men to the ministry. There are some tasks in God's plan that require experience in life that younger men simply cannot handle. This is not to say that older men 'have it all together' in terms of holiness any more than a younger man may. God will always sanctify us and perfect us as we follow Him. There are always areas in our lives to clean up, and many young men can be an example of holiness to people young and old. The example of Abraham, though, does underscore the fact that God has moved and still moves willing and faithful men from one vocation to another.

Maybe you are reading this now and saying to yourself, 'I thought I was too old to serve God. I sense that the Lord is calling me, through His quiet urgings in my own life and through the comments of others, to preach the gospel and shepherd His flock, but I thought that that duty was reserved for younger men.'

I hope you see, through the example of God's dealing with Abraham, that there are simply some jobs in God's kingdom that require a more experienced man or woman. Certainly, the fact of experience does not disqualify you from service. You may be a person like Abram who is called later in life. The story of theological education today is filled with people like you.

MOSES

At first glance, the youthful Moses—a prince in the court of Egyptian royalty, educated in the finest schools of his day—might have seemed like the perfect choice for the ancient equivalent of seminary and full-time ministry to the people of God. But God had to perfect a work in Moses. Moses committed an act of vengeance upon an Egyptian (Exod. 2:11, 12; Acts 7:24, 25). That act of passion cost Moses any opportunity for leadership among his own people (Exod. 2:14), and he went into exile in Midian. There, for forty years, this once proud man with a whole life of service to God before him, lived with only what could have been. He learned to be content with the life of a common herdsman. He learned the importance of family life. He was taught the lessons of the wilderness.

It was the Moses of Midian, and not the Moses of Pharaoh's court, that God called. It is often the case that burning bushes appear to us after wilderness experiences. People who have been 'put on a shelf' by the world are sometimes called into service anew by God.

At the burning bush, Moses heard and responded to God's initial call:

> *'Moses, Moses!'*
> *'Here I am.'*

Yet Moses felt that God had the wrong man:

> *… Who am I that I should go to Pharaoh, and that I should bring the children of Israel out of Egypt? (Exod. 3:11).*

I can relate to this. I felt the same way when I first discerned God's call on my life. After all, Moses had a point, right? A royal rebel who had lost the trust of his own kinsmen (Exod. 2:14) and the favor of the court from which he came, Moses did not think he was a good ministerial candidate. He was an aging man with a resume that included a major identity crisis, manslaughter, and forty years of tending livestock in a two-bit desolate wilderness location. Perhaps you can relate as well.

But even through Moses' act of youthful passion and years of isolation, God had been building a leader. God was calling a man who had learned humility, a man who knew the depths of human depravity and God's grace, a man who knew how to herd a wayward flock in a dangerous wilderness, a man who knew that family wealth was more than mere palaces and jewels, a man who walked with God in the loneliness of his exile.

Burning bushes do not always come when or how we might expect. Burning bushes do not always come *to whom* we might expect—especially when those people include ourselves! But Scripture teaches us that vocations are initiated in the most unlikely places and to the most unlikely candidates.

Some of you who are reading this example of Moses are being called by God to the ordained ministry.[3] Like Moses, you want to say, 'Who am I to go…?'

You look back on your wasted years of youth and think, 'Sure, I could have yielded my life to Christ back then, and could possibly have been a good seminary student and a useful minister of the gospel, but that time is past. I'm forty years old with a spouse and children. After all I've been through, I'm well into my career and feel fortunate just to have a job and rewarding family life. God calling me? That doesn't seem likely.'

---

3   There is a distinct theology of ordination that comes from the Word of God. Ordained speaks to a divine choice to the singularly unique work of priestly ministry of Word and Sacrament.

God replies to those whom He is calling, '… I will certainly be with you…' (Exod. 3:12).

You see, burning bushes do indeed appear to those who are could-have-beens. God calls people who messed up in their earlier years. God even calls them back to the very place where they messed up. God uses those who have learned patience through waiting, who have cultivated a closeness to God through isolation from their past, and who have tended flocks in the back of the desert (Exod. 3:1).

Is that you, dear friend? God has always called such people to His fields of service. Your exile has been your prayer closet. Your wilderness has been your academy. Your 'secular' work has become your sacred witness. You have been under the sovereign hand of Almighty God and didn't even know it. Like Moses, you may be God's chosen one for God's time for God's people.

No young man could have done what Moses did. No young man could have faced a royal court and led a rebellious people through a wilderness to their promised land. Only a seasoned, humbled Moses could have done that. Maybe you too are God's chosen one for God's time for God's people. If He is calling you, you can be sure that you are. You can also be sure that He who calls you will be faithful to equip you and sustain you.

THE DISCIPLES

If the lives of the Old Testament saints who were called to the ordained ministry are not enough to convince you that the older seminarian is nothing new, consider the lives of the New Testament saints. Consider the disciples of Jesus Christ.

In Mark 1:16-20 and Luke 5:2-11 we have the record of the vocational transition of four men: Simon (who was later called Peter); his brother, Andrew; and James and John the sons of Zebedee. As is well known, these men were fishermen. Their transition from professional fishermen and employers (note in Mark 1:20 that they left their business to their employees) to ministers of the gospel of Christ is a further testimony to the way God prepares leaders.

At this point, there are several important observations which might be made which could be of some help to those of you considering a call to ministry:

1. Christ called them while they were faithfully discharging their duties. Mark 1:16 says '... as He walked by the sea of Galilee, He saw Simon and Andrew his brother casting a net into the sea; for they were fishermen.' Simon and Andrew were not monastics waiting on a call. They were not scholars-in-waiting preparing for usefulness in God's kingdom by laying out a strategy for being selected for service. There is nothing wrong with that, of course, and I highly recommend that young men and women who have been identified as candidates for ministry or for missionary service by their local church leaders, begin to prepare for a life of service to Christ. I am simply saying that God, according to His Word, calls some men and women who are busy at their first careers, to leave those careers and follow Him. You are not disqualified from

full-time service to God if your prior education was in preparation for business or a trade. To the contrary.

2. Christ used the disciples' former occupation as a metaphor for service in His kingdom's work. They were fishermen. He told them, 'Follow Me, and I will make you become fishers of men' (Matt. 4:19). So, their first careers were not just written off as wasted time and wasted energy. Their former professions became a living metaphor for service to Christ and His flock. In my own case, I had been a salesman and later a sales manager, as well as a business manager. I remember, in fact, a night I spent tossing and turning in bed. My wife, Mae, told me, 'Honey, you're a salesman. But, God is just showing you that He has a greater product for you to sell.' Some theologians may balk at my lovely wife's remark as demeaning to either the work of the pastor or to the solemnity of the call, but it hit home for me. Her remark validated my work as a salesman and showed me that God had been using my time in secular work to prepare me for sacred work. My lessons in sales, like the disciples' lessons in fishing, would be put to use by the Lord.

Later, my training and experience in management would be put to use in the ministry. I am convinced from God's Word that whether one is a plumber or a salesman or a homemaker or a politician or a farmer, the skills acquired in that first profession are directly transferable to the work of ministry. Your time is not wasted. Jesus meets us on the job, validates our professions and experiences, and employs them for His own blessed designs. God does not, in fact, call all men from the boats. He called only four of them from such on that day when He walked by the Sea of Galilee. Today He is walking in your office and in your factory. He is not calling all of those men and women to leave their work. But He may be calling you. If He is, the Lord will transfer your skills, your tools, your experiences, and even your failures into meaningful metaphors for gospel service.

3. The fishermen left their businesses to become full-time workers for Christ. Mark 1:18 says that 'They immediately left their nets and followed Him.' Not all people are called to do this. I was—and I think many are. It would have been possible, as it was for many who encountered Christ, to follow Him without doing so full-time. But Simon and Andrew and James and John were called to leave their first professions to become full-time laborers with the Savior. There comes a time when one must leave to go to seminary, to leave to prepare for a life of service to Christ and to His flock. Especially for those who are called to the pastorate or to the mission field, the vocation carries with it a requirement to transition from one's former profession to a new one. I am not saying that one cannot work while in seminary or that, like Paul, one might have to 'tent-make' to do ministry, but the overarching focus of one's life becomes Word and Sacrament or evangelism or teaching, not fishing, mending tents, or baking bread. That is a hard step to take. It is admittedly frightening to contemplate leaving a career to follow a call, but if Christ is calling, there is no choice. You will never be happy until you follow Him. He will lead and feed you along the way. The journey from the

fishing boats to the seminary to the parish is filled with serendipitous moments of watching God do miracles. He supplies every need. He, in fact, uses your journey to erect a strong testimony to His faithfulness in your life that you will later share with others.

> *Blessed be the God and Father of our Lord Jesus Christ, the Father of mercies and God of all comfort, who comforts us in all our tribulation that we may be able to comfort those who are in any trouble, with the comfort with which we ourselves are comforted by God.... For all the promises of God in Him are Yes, and in Him Amen, to the glory of God through us. (2 Cor. 1:3-4, 20)*

4.   Note also, in Mark 1:18, that the disciples who followed Jesus left immediately. This is a very serious matter for those called of God. I almost lost my witness at my former vocation because I tried to stay too long. Why? I was sinfully fearful that God wouldn't take care of my family if I left to follow His call. It's called faithlessness, and I had a big case of it. You can't serve God and the world and the flesh at the same time. If God is calling you to the ministry, then be sensible and a good steward of the things entrusted to you on the job, but at the same time, don't tarry. Do what God is calling you to do. It will be better for all.

OUR LORD JESUS CHRIST

Of course, Jesus of Nazareth is our supreme example of the point we argue. Our Lord's own vocational transition is a model for those of us who didn't go to seminary at age twenty-one.

Jesus was a carpenter before He was a preacher. Because He grew in grace with God and man, I would imagine He was, no doubt like Joseph before Him, a renowned craftsman. What ministry skills He must have learned as He studied the grains of wood that He planed, the instruments that He depended on, the grumbling customers that He served, and the satisfaction He enjoyed after completing a project! Jesus was thirty years of age before He would open up and read the lection from Isaiah at the synagogue. He was no longer a boy. He was in His second career: A carpenter-preacher.

As you read this, you may be on your lunch break in a carpentry shop and wondering, If God really is calling you to the ministry, how could He ever use a simple carpenter? Look at your hammer and your auger and your plumb line—these were the primary tools of your Lord, who was the greatest preacher. Whether you labor now in a carpenter shop or a meat market or on the floor of Wall Street, be thankful if God has called you to preach and be assured: you are laboring in a holy place. From such places future sermons, counseling sessions, and outreach campaigns begin.

MINISTRY AS A FIRST CAREER

So far we have discussed the ordained ministry as a second career. Indeed, many of the biblical examples—including the Lord Jesus Christ—focus on ministry as a second career. It is not exclusively so.

In the Old Testament, for example, little Samuel heard the voice of the Lord and with guidance from Eli—

and from his mother—he followed the Lord God from a young age. Timothy, in the New Testament, likewise, was apparently a very young man when he determined to follow the voice of the Lord that he had been taught from a young age by his mother and grandmother. There are clear advantages to following God from a young age as his disciple, just as there are clear advantages to following the Lord in ministry from such a young age.

I'll never forget having a conversation with Dr. D. James Kennedy when I was serving as the interim president of Knox Theological Seminary. We were discussing in various places where I might go to present the seminary as an opportunity for theological training. Dr. Kennedy made it clear to me that he did not want me merely presenting the seminary as a 'brand' to be promoted, but to, firstly, present the gospel of Jesus Christ in order for men and women and boys and girls to be converted and, secondly, to be calling young men and women to missions ministry in various capacities and, thirdly, to call young men to the pastoral ministry (an important support of the statement is that Dr. Kennedy felt that the great work of the seminary president is an evangelist, like Elijah and his school prophets, which I have filled as a personal commitment ever since then). I asked him how *young* did he want me to go? I figured that I would be issuing a call to college-age students. Dr. Kennedy had other ideas. He reminded me that Charles Haddon Spurgeon was simultaneously converted and called to the ministry when he was a teenager. He told me that, as a result, Spurgeon had many more years of ministry productivity because of a younger age of hearing and accepting that pastoral call. Without diminishing the sovereignty of God at all, Dr. Kennedy advocated an urgent presentation of the need for pastors and told me to then trust the Holy Spirit to be the One to call forth those pastors at a tender age. Thus, their training would begin before they even left their homes.

The lesson has stayed with me through all these years. The situation is urgent today. As the Church is moving southward and eastward in its magnificent growth we must be careful to issue the gospel call for missionaries, as well as for pastors—to boys and girls in elementary school as well as in middle school and high school. As revival is sweeping through the continents of Africa and the subcontinent of India, and throughout Asia, and as many are coming to Christ in parts of the Middle East—we will need more pastors to shepherd these emerging flocks. *Now* is the time for us to begin to teach the essential components of the call to pastoral ministry: the inward: the outward call demonstrated and substantiated by the local church, nurtured and trained by an academy accountable to the local church, and apprenticed under another pastor and watchful eye of a superintendent, presbytery, or bishop according to one's own denominational commitments. Theological seminaries are always an outgrowth of the Christian education and missionary movement of the local church. Seminaries are a specialized academic component of the church's mission to prepare the next generation of pastors and missionaries and educators. They often begin within the walls of the church or in other spaces near the church and under the authority of the church. As the academic work is concluded the graduates must return to the church for their residential programs of study. The accrediting relationship with the outside world is good for purposes of accountability, but the single focus is preparing these missionaries, pastors, and educators to shepherd the flock of God and to carry on the great commission in the world today.

4

The Challenges of a Call

At length William Farel detained me at Geneva, not so much by counsel and exhortation, as by a dreadful imprecation, which I felt to be as if God had from heaven laid his mighty hand upon me to arrest me—John Calvin.[1]

The previous chapters discussed what it might mean to hear God's call. But what if you know that you have heard a call? What kinds of things should you think, pray, and seek counsel about as you consider that call?

This chapter speaks to this question, but with two separate kinds of readers in view. The first group includes young people who are still in high school or college. Although these readers might have some work experience in other areas, they are considering ministry as their first career, and thus I will refer to them as 'first-career ministers.' The second group of readers includes those who have chosen a non-ministerial profession in the past

---

1   'Commentary on the Psalms,' vol. 1, Psalms 1-72 (1557), 22.

but are now considering a change that would transform them into 'second-career ministers.'

These labels are not catch-alls; some people pursue two careers at once, a part-time pastorate, or some combination of ministry and other careers that is not fully captured by these two terms. But the basic insight that shapes my reflections below is that different people consider a call at different times of life, and the nature of your personal, family, and professional circumstances at any given time will affect the way you discern God's call for that particular place and time. In what follows, then, I will cover challenges that are often faced by either first-career or second-career ministers. But please remember—these categories are not mutually exclusive! No matter where you fall on this spectrum, I encourage you to read the complete chapter, always keeping in mind the particulars of your own situation and how this might apply to you.

In the first part of the chapter, I will reflect on the question, 'Why don't [more] young men go into the ministry?'

Jesus Christ knew that despite the thrill of following the Creator of the Universe and becoming an official of His Royal Court, an ambassador of the kingdom of the Living God, many would not go into the ministry of His gospel. So, He declared, 'The harvest truly is great, but the laborers are few; therefore pray the Lord of the harvest to send out laborers into the fields' (Luke 10:2).

Today, we are seeing a trend in the ministry. In fact, I think we have a crisis. For a while, in North America, at least, the average age of a seminarian had crept upwards.

This had positive benefits in that older ministers actually begin ministry with accumulated skills and life experiences that can be helpful in Gospel ministry work. Yet, there are downsides. The greatest challenge of older seminarians is time itself. There are fewer years of service remaining. We speak in human terms, of course. God can and will accomplish His will through it all. Well, I am certain there are a number of sociological reasons for a failure of younger candidates to enter ordained ministry. Yet at least one of those reasons is related to the age-old struggle between the one called and the Caller.

The Lord still calls young men into the ordained ministry when they are fifteen, sixteen, and seventeen years of age. But many will not heed the call or will avoid facing the vocation for numerous reasons. Because of misconceptions, these otherwise outstanding candidates for the ministry opt for business and law and medicine and other similar worthy pursuits. Then, ten to fifteen years later—if they are not completely burned-out in their career, which promised them money, prestige, and influence and brought them only dissatisfaction—they begin to reassess their call to ministry.

Now, there are some (and I was one) who are not called until having already established a first career. Why does this happen? Well, for me, it was because my life was so out of order that at twenty years of age, the first call I heard was just to surrender to the grace of God in Christ and trust in Him alone for my eternal life! God would not call me to serve Him until I had believed on His Name.

I am thankful that there are many like me in that regard, many who have received their first call later in life.

But there are other disciples who are faithful even though they are young, and who should be considering God's call to the ministry, but are not. The thing that prevents them from doing so is a set of misconceptions about what matters in life. I believe that many young people today are suffering from a case of mistaken identity—their own!

WHY DON'T YOUNG MEN GO INTO MINISTRY?

Here are some responses that come to mind. These responses are by no means exhaustive and I'm sure you've got some of your own.

Some who are called resist the ministry because they think money will bring them success and happiness. But the truth is, it won't. God's Word teaches this, and many a wealthy person can confirm it from experience. Money is not now, and never will be, a secure path to contentment, strong relationships, or inner peace. If you haven't realized that yet, take a moment to remember: money is not the answer, and a life ordered around the pursuit of money will leave you defeated and disappointed every time.

A life oriented around ministry, however, will be fulfilling and rewarding. The ministry will not normally make you a wealthy man. But, except in extreme cases, it will provide you everything you need in terms of material goods.

The real value of the ministry cannot be measured in currency. What price can be placed on a job that helps people move out of bondage to sin into the freedom offered by Christ? What bonus could you earn that would compare to leading a family to Christ and then holding their children before God as you baptize them before the church? At every important juncture in other people's lives, you are there as the representative and minister of our God. When no one else is allowed to visit, you are permitted to bring a pitcher of living water to thirsty souls and a plate of divine food to those who hunger for something more. Where else can true success and happiness be found?

Some who are called resist the ministry because they think the ministry is boring work. If ministry is nothing more than presiding over set ceremonies, socializing with a few well-to-do parishioners whose tithes keep your kids in braces, and pasting on a smile at community functions in order to bring a few more people out to the annual church maintenance event—if that is what we mean by 'ministry'—then I want out now! What an uninspiring and boring existence.

But that is *not* the ministry, at least not as I know it. That is simply a caricature of the job and is far removed from the reality of day-to-day ministerial life. The reality is that every week—sometimes every day!—something new is happening. It is true that there are some set rhythms: you preach, you teach, you administer the sacraments, you counsel, you administer, you organize, you lead. But within those unchanging rubrics lies a world of diverse operations, a world of difficult assignments, and a world of decisive opportunities! There is certainly nothing *boring* about that.

Allow me to give you a glimpse into just one week in the life of this minister. Within the span of seven days,

I have saved a marriage, led a family to Christ, met with the leaders of my city, offered hope to a grieving family, taught a class on Evidences for the Resurrection, preached a message on the Doctrine of the Sovereignty of God, and dedicated a new building! In what other job can you encounter such an interesting and significant list of activities?

When I think of the ministry, I think of the words of a great preacher who said, 'Do not stoop to be a king when you have been called to preach!' Don't give up something that only appears to be boring because you are allured by something that actually is! The ministry is exciting! If you have any doubts about this, ask someone who has tried it.

Some who are called resist the ministry because they think that ministers are boring people. I can certainly see how this, too, might appear to be the case! I have known some myself (indeed, some have known me to be such)! If the ministry (as Hollywood often portrays it) is carried out by milque-toast, weak-chinned wimps with old, oversized brown cardigan sweaters and a liberal Sunday homily of 'have a nice day,' then I too would find it boring.[2] If ministers are (as some ministers sinfully may be) lazy lugs who do little to contribute to the good of anyone except to the growing size of their pot bellies, then, I would say, 'Yes, ministers are boring people.'

However, I would have you observe history and conclude for yourself if such is really the case. Consider

2   I remember my friend John Guest telling me that he resisted the ministry because of the same reason until he heard Billy Graham preaching the Gospel in the London crusade on March 1, 1954.

the prophets of the Old Testament. No one reading the life of the minor prophet Amos could honestly assert that he was a boring individual. A simple man called from herding sheep and tending sycamore fruit to preaching to royalty in an apostate kingdom is hardly leading a boring life. Risky? Yes. Influential? Yes. But never boring. The same goes for Moses, Abraham, David, Isaiah, Jeremiah and the rest of those stalwart men of God.

Consider the apostles. Whether we consider Peter, who went from being a middle-class fisherman to an emboldened preacher to thousands; or Thomas, who went from being the skeptic who fell before the risen Christ to the one who, according to tradition, brought the gospel to India; or numerous others who gave their lives away for a cause greater than themselves; we are speaking of the very personages who changed the world. Time spent with them would not have left us looking for something better to do.

I also draw your attention to the 'least of the apostles.' For the apostle Paul, following Christ into the ministry meant leaving a career. It meant, for him, facing the very people whom he once persecuted. What a risk! What a change! But Paul went forward in spite of this, and in the hands of God, he became a catalyst that literally changed the course of human history. When historians trace the diverse tributaries of world history through Western civilization, the streams begin to merge at the living waters flowing from the consecrated ministry and recorded letters of one changed man: Saul of Tarsus.

Consider the Reformers. We have mentioned Luther previously, but what of Calvin? If you do a little research, you will find that this one Frenchman has influenced not only theology but also politics and economics. Can we truly speak of modern history without mentioning Wycliffe and the translation of the Word of God into English? My dear friends, there is every evidence that ministers of the gospel have had as much if not more influence on the lives of even the most disinterested modern man or woman as merchants and scientists and artists.

Consider the founders of our nation's institutions. We cannot speak of the great institutions of higher education without acknowledging the role of ordained ministers. All of the great Ivy League schools were founded by ministers, and many of what became state universities were founded by the clergy. But, if we went further and asked who influenced the great businessmen in our nation, would we not begin to list countless ministers of every Christian denomination across the globe?

Consider the leaders of the great social changes in our own country. Whether we are speaking of the movement to overturn slavery or to advance civil rights for minorities or to protect the rights of children and the elderly and the unborn, we will be bound to name the names of famous ministers of the gospel who led the charge.

Some of you reading this live in countries in the continent of Africa. Others of you live in the Western nations, while yet others live in parts of Asia. There were pastors and other Christian leaders in each of our respective nations who took stands for righteousness. All of us can think of pastors, missionaries and evangelists around the world who stood up for the sake of Jesus Christ or for the sake of injustice. Some of the most courageous figures in world history were not only Christians but were Christian leaders who inspired the rest of the church and, in many cases, the rest of the world.

No, ministers are not boring people. Some ministers are just bad ministers. They want to be influential, and they think that the ministry is not. Again, this is a misconception born out of poor ministers and bad Hollywood scripts.

If you want to influence society, be a minister. You can change lives in a local church as a pastor or associate pastor. You can mold lives in a Christian school, college, or seminary as a teacher, professor, or headmaster. You can travel to unreached people groups and change the course of a whole nation for the rest of history as a missionary. You can change this nation as a church planter.

There is no greater joy than changing one life at a time with the simple news of Jesus Christ—His grace, His atoning sacrifice, His invitation to a new life.

Ministers have been and continue to be the most influential members of society at both the personal level, and in many cases, the national and even world level.

FACING THE TRUTH

The real question is, will you face the truth of the ministry as it is, or will you hold on to your misconceptions? To hold on to your misconceptions is to rule out the ministry as a viable option for you.

To get real with it, though, is to get risky. It is a risk to give your life up to Jesus Christ and the service of His kingdom. There is no doubt about it—ministry *is* risky. But what great thing has ever been done without risk?

I was once frightened of this very thing. I thought that if I gave my life to Christ and to His service, I would be in chains forever. Bored and boring, I would labor in vain in a field that was never ripe for harvest.

I then read Edmund Clowney's book *Called to the Ministry*, and I came across something very interesting. Martin Luther, the great Reformer, must have felt the same way as I did. In fact, Luther had been given the gifts to become one of the greatest legal minds in all of Europe. Luther was additionally blessed with exceptional gifts in music and might have enjoyed a status on par with the greatest musicians of Germany. But, he was called to the ministry. He said that his call to preach and to teach and to be an ambassador for Jesus Christ had become burdensome to him! Perhaps Luther, too, was confused as to whether he should pursue these other outstanding fields, but in the end, he could not, because he knew he had to give his life to the ministry of the gospel of Jesus Christ. The ministry had become chains to him. But these were not chains of death. Luther was saying, 'In my chains, I at last found my freedom.'

That is the way I felt. I embraced the chains of the gospel. Paul's credo became my own: 'Woe is me if I preach not the Gospel!' (1 Cor. 9:16). In those chains, I have found the greatest freedom I have ever known.

If you are a young person who has not yet committed to a career path in life, I encourage you to consider whether God may be calling you to the ministry. I encourage some others of you to consider whether God might be calling you to some other form of Christian service. Are you allowing any misconceptions about the ministry to hold you back?

Jesus said in a parable, 'Why have you been standing here all day long doing nothing?' And the unemployed laborers answered, 'Because no one has hired us.' He said to them, 'You also go and work in my vineyard.'

How many young people will heed the call? How many will stretch forward their neck and hands and take the yoke of Christ upon them as a minister of the gospel? How many will find the greatest freedom and fulfillment that young or old has ever known?

The Word of God and God's acts in history confirm that He calls people of all stations of life and at all phases of life. This includes the second-career minister. And while there is no doubt that God calls older individuals into full-time ministry, it is also the case that answering such a call has its own unique challenges.

ECONOMICS

The first difficulty faced by those called from a first career into the ministry is economic in nature. Usually adults at this point have a family and a mortgage. The God who requires that we give priority to our families and their needs in this life never violates one of His commandments by issuing another, such as a call to ministry. If you are called to preach the gospel, my friend, you must do so and take care of your family as you do. This is not impossible, but it is a tremendous undertaking that will call on your resourcefulness and dedication to both your family and your vocation.

When God called me to preach, I had a wife, a teenage daughter, and a ninety-three-year-old aunt to care for. God, of course, knew this when He called me, so when I prayed that He take care of my problem, He gave me a job to support my family while in seminary. I had left home and career and friends to go off and prepare for a life of preaching. Many of you who read this will do the same and so have many before us. The Lord promises that for those who are called to follow Him at personal expense He will repay your losses and more in this life and the next.

I shall never forget the day I told my boss that I was leaving to go to seminary. He (an unbeliever) told me, 'Well, I can't say I understand it, but it does seem a natural thing for you to do.' Then, he said, 'Well, Mike, what can we do to help you? Will you need a job?' I thought I was going to drop right there. After regaining my composure, I replied, 'I guess ... why, yes! Of course!' The next day he called me and said, 'I think this God of yours must be on your side. It looks like the man who hired you into the company eight years ago is now the regional manager over the Southeast. I told him that you were going to go to seminary in Florida. He has a job opening for a salesman in Miami, and it's yours if you want it.'

In just a few days, we were on our way to south Florida, headed to Knox Seminary and to my new job. God honored His Word as we yielded to Him. I have never experienced the power of God more than at those times in our lives.

Yes, living is going to take money, but God has all the money in the world. If you need a job, anticipate that God will open the door. Furthermore, treat your seminary experience as a mission, because it is. Ask your church leadership to help represent your needs to the congregation. It is important to take care of your family's financial and material needs at any point in life, and you should not neglect this. But take heart that God also knows about these needs, and seek Him for the best steps to take in order to be sure they are met.

Then wait. God is about to move to provide your every need according to His riches in glory (Phil. 4:19).

Family

I was very busy during the years I was in seminary. I was a full-time student with a full-time job *and* an internship. I don't recommend that for everyone, but it can be done. I'll admit that there was little free time and plenty of rushed breakfasts and late nights, but with the cooperation of the whole family, a short-term mission such as this can be carried out.

One important thing to remember is that this season of life is temporary. That doesn't mean that you should neglect your family life, but simply that you have to see this season for what it is. My wife and I were very intentional about family time during those years (and still are). For Mae and me, Saturday mornings were sacred. We would go for a walk and then go to a mall and walk around together. Sometimes we might picnic. Sometimes we snuggled as we went up and down the aisles of Wal-Mart. This was our seminarian's Sabbath.

I owe my wife, Mae, a great debt for managing many aspects of our lives during those seminary years. There is no doubt that you, too, will need not only divine assistance but spousal assistance as well. If you have children, to the degree that they are of age to understand what is going on, include them as well in the planning and decision-making regarding how best to spend time together as a family. Your own parents or extended family members may also have a role to play in organizing holiday celebrations, vacations, or daily life (depending on their location) in ways that support the growth and health of your family even while you are very busy with the commitments of training for ministry.

The primary message I want to convey here is: take care of your family. Think about how best to sustain these relationships even under the strain of the necessary requirements. And remember, seminary is a training ground not only in the classroom, but in all of life. There will not be *fewer* demands on your time, mind, or emotional energy when you become a minister. Now is the time to learn how to carve out moments for nurturing the important human relationships in your life.

HEALTH

The work of ministry is physically rigorous. It's more than carrying heavy textbooks that gets you, though! The tasks of going to seminary, working a job, caring for family life, and possibly even maintaining a yard can sap all your strength and leave you physically exhausted.

No matter your age, I recommend a thorough physical prior to coming to seminary. God is not asking you to ruin your health. If you're not up to it, you may want to rethink how you can pull off seminary. It may be a matter of attending to your health *before* entering seminary. Or you may need to discuss how your new living arrangement (commute time, level of house/yard care, etc.) will impact your time at seminary. What worked well while you were in another career might not work now. These are all issues to think about, pray about, and talk about with those who love you.

For the average middle-aged person, the physical demands of seminary life (and preparation for ministry) will be manageable, but we must also consider our health as we count the cost of service to Christ. Consider your strengths and weaknesses in this area as you evaluate the nature of God's call on your life at this point in your personal and professional journey.

SPIRITUAL OPPOSITION TO THE SEMINARIAN

We know the ways of the enemy of God's people:

> *Be sober-minded; be watchful. Your adversary the devil prowls around like a roaring lion, seeking someone to devour (1 Pet. 5:8, ESV).*

The devil is always seeking to do war with the saints who can best advance the work of God.

So the dragon was enraged with the woman, and went off to make war with the rest of her children, who keep the commandments of God and hold to the testimony of Jesus (Rev. 12:17, NASB).

The seminarian is one 'red-meat' child of God targeted by Satan, for the seminarian will be a preacher who will declare the unsearchable riches of Jesus Christ. That message will be potent and will germinate into a thousand generations of Christians populating heaven throughout eternity. That seminarian will one day declare a Christ whose word will liberate lives from the grip of Hell and the destiny of the devil. Thus, the time of preparation in the life of the past would be an intense time of spiritual warfare. The best antidote for this diabolical front will be the study of the word in prayer, the sacrament of the Lord's supper, regular worship, the fellowship of the saints, being in the Spirit on the Lord's Day with the people of God, so that your season of learning is a veritable walking with God in the garden.

THE OPEN DOOR BEFORE YOU

I cannot say anything to you that is more important than this: today you may be a laborer in the country of Wales, you may be a factory worker in China, or a businessman in Berlin, or a fisherman in Alaska, but the burden you may be experiencing concerning the ministry is, quite possibly, not repelling you but drawing you. You sense that the struggle is leading you to follow. You have come to believe that you will not be happy in any work but declaring Christ within the narrow channels of word, sacrament, and prayer in the parish ministry. Perhaps, you recognize that you are drawn to a mission, even to a singular geographic location, or to a classroom. God is calling you to the ministry of preparation for so great a call.

RESPONDING TO A CALL

As you discern the nature of God's call, you are probably doing some additional Bible study and spending time in prayer. You may have come to the end of what you believe you can know on your own and begun to seek godly counsel. This is good!

Whether you are a first-career or second-career minister, I hope you can see that God calls all kinds of people at all phases of life into ministry. This chapter will address the question of what to do when it is time to respond to God's call. This is the case whether you have discovered that the Lord is *not* calling you into professional ministry at this time, or whether He *is*.

GO BACK TO YOUR HOME AND TELL OTHERS: WHEN GOD SAYS 'NO' TO THE ORDAINED MINISTRY

You may have discovered through a process of sifting that you are not called into ordained ministry at this time. Now, you are faced with the weighty matter of putting legs on your theology. It is time to return to your initial vocation with a renewed sense of purpose. Return to your home church with a refreshed zeal for serving Christ in those several and sundry ministry opportunities available to you there.

Consider a model case in the Bible in which God's call was something different than the person in question desired:

> *And when He got into the boat, he who had been demon-possessed begged Him that he might be with Him. However, Jesus did not permit him, but said to him, 'Go home to your friends, and tell them what great things the Lord has done for you, and how He has had compassion on you.' And he departed and began to proclaim in Decapolis all that Jesus had done for him; and all marveled. (Mark 5:18-20)*

We have here a man, the Gadarene demoniac, who had been healed and transformed by Christ. His immediate response? He wants to leave his environment and follow Jesus in humble service.

But Jesus responded with a 'no.' Instead, He called this passionate, grateful fellow to remain with family and friends and neighbors and share the compassion of the Lord with them. In doing so, he could reach people who might otherwise never encounter the truth of the gospel.

And so, the healed demoniac did just that. The Bible says, 'And all marveled.' His ministry was not cut off, but expanded. He was still able to testify to God's grace and healing. This is the promise given to those who have been told, 'No, my son, your calling is not to the ordained ministry.'

Every person is a person of worth and value before God. Sometimes, that is difficult for us to understand. We have the tendency, at such times and in such cases, to think that our ministry is somehow of less use to God if it is occasional or paired with other professional activities. But, although the transformed demoniac was not to be one of the twelve, he had a powerful ministry in Decapolis. We, too, may be powerfully used of God in circumstances other than that of ordained ministry.

Consider, also, the clear teaching of St. Paul:

For as we have many members in one body, but all the members do not have the same function, so we, being many, are one body in Christ, and individually members of one another. Having then gifts differing according to the grace that is given to us, let us use them: if prophecy, let us prophesy in proportion to our faith; or ministry, let us use it in our ministering; he who teaches, in teaching; he who exhorts, in exhortation; he who gives, with liberality; he who leads, with diligence; he who shows mercy, with cheerfulness. (Rom. 12:4-8)

The Apostle speaks of 'gifts differing according to the grace that is given to us ....' He then lists several, but surely, not every gift. If you have received a negative response to your query about becoming a minister, the weighty matter for you now is to consider the depth of your passion, your experience, and your service to Jesus Christ and to His people. The outcome of those considerations will become the gifts of God, through your life, to us, the church.

If you are one who has listened for the voice of the Lord and has heard, 'No, my child, to the ordained ministry'; then you will soon hear, 'This way, my little one.' As Eli instructed Samuel, 'Go...if He calls you...say, "Speak, Lord, for Your servant hears"' (1 Sam. 3:9).

May you hear your name spoken clearly: 'It is the Lord. Let Him do what seems good to Him'(1 Sam. 3:18).

73

May you serve joyfully, with a full heart, and with all of the love and commitment that inspired your inquiry into ministry in the first place.

THE PATHWAY: WHEN GOD SAYS 'YES,' GOD SAYS, 'GO'

I will now address my remarks for those of you who, like Samuel, have heard the Lord and believe with Paul that 'Woe is me' if you do not follow Christ as an ordained minister. For you, too, we must repeat the admonition of Eli:

> It is the LORD. Let Him do what seems good to Him. (1 Sam. 3:18)

Now is the time to survey the road ahead. Now is the time to count the cost of obedience. If God has called you to the ordained ministry—as best as you can determine through the process described previously—then it is, indeed, time to begin the process ... and it is a process, as we shall see.

Before I go further, I want to take what I suspect is a very necessary diversion to a different but related matter. Spiritual landmines are placed, it seems, at every turn in the process of responding to a call, whether you are early in life or considering a career change. Probably the first one you will encounter is set by your own self-interests, and the potentially disabling instrument is nestled deep in your own soul.

URGENCY: LET THE DEAD BURY THEIR DEAD (OR, WHY IT IS BEST TO GET ON WITH IT)

What is the landmine? It's the matter of putting the call off. If you are discerning a second-career call, you may be familiar with the sensation of procrastination. Not a small number of older seminarians are making a mid-career transition because they refused to act on God's call to them earlier in life. Thus, when they face the matter once more, they must face the same old demons. What are you to do?

Plain and simple, if you are called, waste no time. Get on with it.

Yes, I know you have responsibilities at your company or organization. We'll get into that later. Yes, I know you have a family. God knows that and is already dealing with the souls of your precious loved ones if He is calling you. In fact, many times, they knew it before you did!

Yes, I know you don't have all of your bills paid off and you wanted to wait to go to seminary after you were in better financial shape. Yes, I know…and God knows.

But, the fact is this: either you are called to the ordained ministry or you are not. If you are called (and you have worked through that process of identifying the outward and inward call and have sought counsel from others who have encouraged you in this), then you must simply go. The matter before you is the matter of urgency.

I know about all of these things because I was there. I knew I was called to the ministry. My wife knew I was called. The problem was, I was locating each and every reason why I should not go to seminary and was offering them up to God, hoping He would buy it.

He didn't.

I remember the day I was making a sales call, if memory serves me well, in Dublin, Ohio. I was in my rental car and, as usual, had tuned in to find a local Christian radio station. Hoping to hear some soothing music to quiet my troubled soul at that time (troubled, again, over the matter of when to go and how to do it), I could find only a preacher. 'As it happened' (a favorite way that the scriptures introduce pivotal events), the minister, a local preacher, was preaching on Luke 9 and a very familiar passage:

> *Now it happened as they journeyed on the road, that someone said to Him, 'Lord, I will follow you wherever You go.' And Jesus said to him, 'Foxes have holes and birds of the air have nests, but the Son of Man has nowhere to lay His head.' Then He said to another, 'Follow Me.' But he said, 'Lord, let me first go and bury my father.' Jesus said to him, 'Let the dead bury their own dead, but you go and preach the kingdom of God.' And another also said, 'Lord, I will follow You, but let me first go and bid them farewell who are at my house.' But Jesus said to him, 'No one, having put his hand to the plow, and looking back, is fit for the kingdom of God.' After these things the Lord appointed seventy others also, and sent them two by two before His face into every city and place where He Himself was about to go. Then He said to them, 'The harvest truly is great, but the laborers are few; therefore pray the Lord of the harvest to send out laborers into His harvest.' (Luke 9:57-10:2).[3]*

That passage, through the power of the Spirit, changed my life.

In the story, Jesus issues a call for laborers to go out into the harvest and proclaim the kingdom of God in Christ. There is urgency resounding in the whole text. The Lord,

---

3   See also Matthew 8:19-22.

knowing the heart of mankind,[4] reminded His eager followers about the cost of service. There is an uncertainty to the ministry and a built-in opposition to it in this age that can potentially render you even without a home or a pillow! This is the cost of accepting this call. Yet, if you are compelled by a call resonating in the deepest parts of your soul, then you must respond, also at great cost, to the Lord of the Harvest.

The problem with one of the people Jesus addresses is that he is not quite ready. He has to go and bury his father. The great New Testament scholar, A. T. Robertson, handles it this way:

> *The burial of one's father was a sacred duty (Gen. 25:9), but, as in the case of Tobit 4:3, this scribe's father probably was still alive. What the scribe apparently meant was that he could not leave his father while still alive to follow Jesus around over the country.... The explanation is that the spiritually dead can bury the literally dead.... The harshness of this proverb to the scribe probably is due to the fact that he was manifestly using his aged father as an excuse for not giving Christ active service. But go thou and publish abroad the kingdom of God. The scribe's duty is put sharply.... Christ called him to preach, and he was using pious phrases about his father as a pretext. Many a preacher has had to face a similar delicate problem of duty to father, mother, brothers, sisters and the call to preach. This was a clear case. Jesus will help any man called to preach to see his duty. Certainly Jesus*

---

4   'But Jesus did not commit Himself to them, because He knew all men, and had no need that anyone should testify of man, for He knew what was in man' (John 2:24, 25).

does not advocate renunciation of family duties on the part of preachers.[5]

The radio preacher didn't put it quite like old Dr. Robertson, but he interpreted it in precisely the same spirit.

The message hit me like a brick.

I pulled my rental car over to the side of the highway. 'Lord, you got me.' I knew the man in the passage was none other than me, and I knew the Lord of the Harvest was making it ever so clear. 'I have called you. Go. Now. I know you have other responsibilities. Take care of them. I'll help. But, don't use them as excuses. Let the dead bury the dead, but you follow Me.'

When I returned home, I told my wife, and I committed to leave all and follow the call. As it turned out, it took one more year before everything was in place for forward progress, but that was God's business, not mine. There were several issues that had to be resolved, and God took them firmly in hand. The delay was not due to my stalling. I had committed myself to the pathway He had laid out, and He would take care of the rest.

I never experienced greater peace than I did during those days.

So, if you are called, yield your life to the Lord and get ready. God is about to do some wonderful things in your life.

---

5 *Word Pictures in the New Testament*, Volume II, 'The Gospel According to Luke,' Archibald Thomas Robertson (New York: Harper and Brothers Publishers, 1930), 141.

Decency and Order: The Ruling Motif in the Process of Accepting the Call

As stated, there's no place for waiting around or dragging your feet once you are sure of your call. But at the same time, it's not up to you to determine what the next steps are.

Yes, your call comes from God. But that call comes to you through the church (via the outward call) and must be validated by the church (via counseling from your pastor and lay leadership and, possibly, from a middle judicatory, such as a presbytery, diocese, association, or district). Your response to that call also must be supervised by the church.

The apostle Paul, who started his epistles by underscoring the divine nature of his call,[6] is the same apostle Paul who, after his calling, was brought by Barnabas to the other apostles:

> *But Barnabas took him and brought him to the apostles. And he declared to them how he had seen the Lord on the road, and that He had spoken to him, and how he had preached boldly at Damascus in the name of Jesus (Acts 9.27).*

---

6 Note Paul's constant appeal to his call tethered to God's will: '... through the will of God...' in 1 Corinthians 1:1; '... by the will of God...' in 2 Corinthians 1:1; most pointedly in Galatians 1:1, 'Paul, an apostle (not from men nor through man, but through Jesus Christ and God the Father who raised Him from the dead) ...'; 'by the will of God' in Ephesians 1:1; '...by the will of God...' in Colossians 1:1; '...by the commandment of God our Savior and the Lord Jesus Christ, our hope...' in 1 Timothy 1:1 and 'I thank Christ Jesus our Lord who has enabled me, because He counted me faithful, putting me into the ministry...' in 1 Timothy 1:12; '...by the will of God...' in 2 Timothy 1:1.

This is a vitally important point for you to remember at this juncture. Your calling must be from God, but that will not allow one to act independently of God's church. Like Paul, our gifts and our calling and the practice of our ministry are under the oversight of the church. There should be no loose cannons in the church. Order and decency, so vital in worship, are also necessary for ministry preparation.

What Now?

The answer to that question will be provided, usually, by the church. A great deal of the particulars depends upon the denomination; yet there are a number of similarities across denominations. All require some level of formal education, whether that be an undergraduate degree, graduate program, a series of internships, or supervised mentoring. These are details to be looked into with your own pastor, mentor, or denominational leaders.

But no matter what the formal requirements are, the following fundamental values are important touchstones as you respond to a call.

If the call is so great, shouldn't the preparation be equal to the vocation? I happen to believe that the answer to that is self-evident. The call to ordained ministry is great. It is, really, a gift. God is the Giver, and the call to preach means there is a resident gift of preaching along with other gifts. Thus, unto whom much is given much is required.[7]

---

7   'For everyone to whom much is given, from him much will be required; and to whom much has been committed, of him they will ask the more' (Luke 12:48b).

When God called me, I remember thinking that if He were to give me thirty years of ministry (and at my age then, that was a reasonable possibility), my commitment to invest three good years in preparation would be simply my tithe to God for the gift of ministry He had given to me. I determined, then, that I would seek the very best academic and practical training I could get in order to prepare for the gospel ministry.

It is sometimes tempting to want to rush through the preparation in order to get to the action of ministry as quickly as possible. It is a good thing to desire a good ministry. But part of developing and sustaining a life of ministry is investing in preparation. Take seriously your denomination's requirements in this regard, and prayerfully seek where and how you can grow in the faith during the years of preparation set before you.

The call may be clear, but that doesn't't mean you can forsake your present career. This is particularly the case for second-career ministers. I almost tripped over this point.

There is an art to leaving. Shakespeare, writing in *Macbeth*, made this observation:

> *Nothing in his life*
> *Became him like the leaving it; he died*
> *As one that had been studied in his death*
> *To throw away the dearest thing he ow'd*
> *As 'twere a careless trifle.*[8]

---

8   *Macbeth*, Act I, Scene iv, 7.

While this is said of one who left this world for eternity, may it be said of those who leave a career to follow God's call.

For some of you this will not be leaving a career, but leaving a career planned for you by your parents. John Calvin faced this. Calvin's father prepared him for a career in law. Yet he found that he was being steered into ministry. There is a way to honor your mother and your father—indeed, you must—as you explain the call upon your life to follow your Lord. There is a way to do so with a graciousness that shows respect. I counseled one young Indian Army officer whose parents were very proud of him. When he told them that he wanted to go to graduate school they were very supportive. They had planned for him to pursue his MBA at Harvard or Yale. When he told them that he was not pursuing a business degree but in fact a divinity degree in preparation for a life as a minister of the gospel their excitement withered. The young man came to me and through prayer and patience we devised a response that sought to honor the parents and to honor God. It wasn't perfect but in the end he found a way to go to a school that they could respect, close to them—and he had not been near to them for 10 years—and yet prepare himself for the ordained ministry in his particular denomination. With prayer, patience, wise counsel, and love there is always a way through the barriers of misunderstanding.

HOW TO LEAVE YOUR CAREER WITH INTEGRITY
The issue is very relevant to the pursuit of the call. First, your leaving is a testimony to God's activity in your life.

The way you handle it will speak to others about the reality of God! If you handle it poorly, many will assume that the whole business of ministry and church is a sham—something less committed to excellence than the marketplace. Alternatively, if you leave well, they just may get interested in this God who calls.

As I related at the end of the last chapter, I came close to tripping at this juncture. I was waiting too long. I was dealing with the 'let the dead bury the dead' issues and, meanwhile, allowing the complicated emotional charges (and all which that entails) to detonate at work. In short, while doing a great deal of pre-seminary study and reading, I was not giving everything I could on the job. Furthermore, I knew that at some time I would leave and therefore was letting up without realizing it.

Now, I am not advocating irresponsible behavior at this point. Prior to seminary, particularly for those with family, one must do everything possible to secure income and take care of the needs of those within your care, as well as tuition and moving expenses. What I am advocating is this: if God has called you, don't ride on the back of your employer too long. Let them know. Be forthright. Don't sneak around. Develop a plan and watch God do the rest.

Now many of your co-workers and friends and well-meaning relatives will tell you that you are crazy. If in fact you are highly successful in your present career, this fact only adds to their suspicion that you are crazy. 'Why are you throwing it all away? Can't you serve God at the firm?' Well, yes. We dealt with that earlier in the theology of vocation. But, you have been called to the ministry of Word and Sacrament. You will have to be patient with them. It probably took several years for God to get through to you, so be as longsuffering with others as God was with you! Most of them will come around. Some of them will even come to faith in Christ in all of this. Others, probably a minority, will sulk about this for a long, long time. Why? Because your decision to leave a career—a successful career—and follow a call strikes at their decision—probably many years earlier—*not* to do it. You are living out their forfeited dreams. Secretly, they will even respect you. Pray for them. Love them. Treat them the way God treated you—with mercy and grace.

It's time to go and prepare for your call.

You are called to the ordained ministry. You are also, probably, a successful farmer, a student preparing for law, a salesman, manager, teacher, computer programmer, or a craftsman in an apprenticeship program. So, how do you make the move with integrity, in a way that maintains your witness to Christ?

This is all part of responding to the call. Don't rush ahead too far, and don't turn away too quickly from the commitments God has already given you.

Having been called by God it remains for all of us to put our affairs in order and to follow the Lord Jesus. He speaks a universal word that is particularized. And He speaks a particular word that must be expressed in the universal. So we are called from our singular locations and perhaps even preparations for another career to follow Him to seminary—that may be a graduate school of theology in the United Kingdom or North America or an apprenticeship in Africa or Bible college in Taiwan or a community study toward ordained ministry in an underground church in the Middle East. Yet it is always a call to immerse in the Word, Sacrament, and Prayer. And it is a call to prepare. That is our next chapter.

5

Selecting a Seminary

There is a great biblical precedent of preparing for the gospel ministry. The Old Testament provides a model with Elijah and the school of the prophets. The New Testament provides the model with Jesus and His disciples. The apostle Paul and Timothy are another model. The apostle Paul himself is a model as he testifies about his time of three years in Arabia to prepare for ministry. The rabbinical tradition within the Jewish church, from which Christianity sprang, is an institution, out of which our Lord was, at least, nurtured, and, which certainly produced Saul of Tarsus. The school of rabbinical tradition was steeped in the instruction of Torah, the prophets, and the writings. The school was set within a framework of structured mentorships, liturgical training, prophetic voice, parishioner relationships, and many other aspects of the pastoral work (e.g., the school of Gamaliel)[1]. From

---

1   See, e.g., a survey of the ancient rabbinical schools, from the pre-Mishnaic period, in Menachem Mansoor, *Jewish History*

this rich tradition the Christian church has built upon the biblical doctrine of vocation and the scriptural example of pastoral training to build the academic architecture of theological higher education. To use the phrase 'theological higher education' is not to be exclusively Western. We may, for example, look to African expressions of theological higher education or Asian or Latin American expressions and find rich variations that cultivate and even reform the educational ministry of the church. Instead it is to say that there exists a distinct theological higher education ministry within the church that in places may be a part of the Western system of colleges and universities and may, simultaneously, be expressed in apprenticeship programs in other branches of the church. This in no way detracts from either the effectiveness nor the validity of one or the other. Indeed, it should be stressed, the singular parts work together to enrich the whole. Organizations such as the Lausanne Movement and the International Council for Evangelical Theological Education do laudable work in leading us to see the great need for global theological education in our day. Indeed, we are facing a great crisis of training pastors in our world:

> More than 2.2 million pastoral leaders (and as many as 3.4 million by some estimates) presently minister, while 'only 5% are trained for pastoral ministry' according to the Center for the Study of Global Christianity. Thus more than 2 million pastoral leaders need immediate strengthening for their pastoral ministries. Further, if a pastoral leader is able

---

and Thought: An Introduction (Hoboken, New Jersey: Ktav Pub. House, 1991), 138ff.

initially to provide pastoral care for a group of 50 believers, 1,000 new pastors are daily needed to serve the 50,000 new believers baptized every day. We are rather behind. How may we quicken the pace of pastoral training (a challenge to formal pastoral training models) while increasing the quality (a challenge to ad-hoc, non-formal pastoral training initiatives) everywhere?[2]

So the larger issue of theological education for those called is a great issue before us. Yet I know that there is a more personalized matter before you: what shall you do?

HOW DO YOU CHOOSE A SEMINARY?

Now I realize for many of you the issue of the selection of a seminary is a moot issue, because so many of you will have only one choice. For others, particularly those in North America and in the British Isles and continental Europe—and some in Latin America—there will be the opportunity for choice in one's theological education. As I address important variables in making that decision I hope I will also touch on some matters that will be important to all of you. Even if you don't have a choice in theological education I believe that the issues I address will be of importance to you in preparing for your pastoral preparation. While there are many variables that we could examine, let's focus on these six:

- affinity with your own denominational commitments;
- doctrinal integrity;

2   Ramesh Richardson, 'Training of Pastors—Lausanne Movement,' Lausanne Movement, July 08, 2015, accessed October 10, 2015, http://www.lausanne.org/content/lga/2015-09/training-of-pastors

- faculty commitments;
- academic excellence;
- resources;
- and residency-internship opportunities.

Affinity

Before going too deeply into the selection of a seminary, you should consider your denomination's requirements, as well as your local judicatory. Some associations, presbyteries, districts, and dioceses allow their candidates to go to seminaries outside of their jurisdiction (and increasingly, outside of their theological tradition). So, the first thing to do is to discuss the options with your denominational representative.

Once you have that information in hand, there are several criteria that I would suggest you use in your evaluation of which seminary to select. Keep these in mind as you review their websites, talk to current students and faculty, plan a campus visit, or speak with admissions staff.

Doctrinal Integrity

It is important to choose a seminary that is faithful to the message God has called you to proclaim. This doesn't mean, of course, that you should not be challenged in your beliefs or have your horizons broadened as to what others believe. You should be challenged. This might also help you understand the perspectives of visitors to your church or of those who don't share your doctrinal commitments. Yet, it is equally clear that if you are a Calvinist and choose to go to Asbury Theological Seminary because you happen to live in Wilmore, Kentucky, you may experience extreme theological discomfort (since Asbury, a very fine Wesleyan school, is decidedly *not* Calvinistic!). The same would be true for a convinced Wesleyan who wanted to serve in the Church of the Nazarene and decided to attend Reformed Theological Seminary. Now, each of these would get a superior theological education, to be sure, but within the context of competing traditions. Unless you are convinced that God is calling you to test your convictions, I would advise attending a graduate school that has some theological proximity to your own basic convictions.

FACULTY COMMITMENT

As one who has led a seminary, taught in a seminary, and counseled and recruited seminary students, I have often stated that if I had a godly, thoroughly committed, and highly student-driven faculty, I could start a seminary in a hotel room and 'they would come.'

Your choice of a seminary to prepare you for the ministry must include a thorough examination of the faculty. Your professors are your mentors and your mentors should be pastor-scholars. Your concept of God, of the church, of your role in the ministry is, to a great degree, if not derived from, at least, informed by and shaped through the vision and commitment of the faculty under whom you will train. The pastoral degree is a professional degree and, as such, it is a formation degree, not a research degree. This is a time in which you will be molded to begin to look like the one who trains you.

What should you look for? I would look for a commitment to the scriptures and to the historic, classical confessions of the Church. You, of course, can locate that easily enough in the institutional mission statement. The proof of the pudding, though, will be in the individual commitment of the professors.

How, then, do you make such a determination, given that in most cases you won't know the faculty personally until you enroll and study with them? Good starting places include reading their publications, talking to former or current students, and sitting in on a class or conducting a formal interview with one or two of them during your application process. Knowing what and where they publish is one sign of their commitments, but so too is knowing when and how they have served in a ministerial context. It is one thing to write about church leadership and another to participate in it. Both of these have a role to play in the church, but it's important to understand the difference.

When God called me to preach, my wife and I determined that we would go to the best school possible in order to prepare for a life of preaching and service in the church. We felt the call demanded such a commitment on our part. Our decision to attend a seminary that was just beginning[3] was largely made by our personal interviews with the professors. Again, I don't advise choosing a graduate school of theology based upon the age of the ivy on the brick, but by the relationship of the seminary to the Vine. Jesus said, 'I am the vine, you are the branches.

---

3   Knox Theological Seminary, Fort Lauderdale, Florida in 1990.

He who abides in Me, and I in him, bears much fruit; for without Me you can do nothing' (John 15:5).

ACADEMIC EXCELLENCE

Choose a school that combines academic excellence with a commitment to praxis—that is, practice. One without the other is no good. Over and over you will hear from preachers who say, 'My seminary was academic, but not practical,' or 'My school really stressed the practical, but I feel I didn't get an education.' Look for a balance in this area, for both elements are essential for your training.

'That which we have seen and heard we declare unto you' (1 John 1:3) is an important scripture to meditate upon when considering a seminary. Have these professors, my prospective mentors, experienced the ministry on the front lines to such a degree that they are able to integrate scholarship with praxis? And, are the internship or practical requirements of the curriculum supported by a strong reading and research element?

The question is not just, 'have they published?' but, especially, 'have they preached?' Demand both. This will stand you in good stead in the years ahead.

RESOURCES

The physical and technical resources that most seminaries have prior to being accredited are self-evident (books, computers, etc.). Much could also be written, of course, about the availability of resources such as Logos and other such online Bible and theological education material, as well as Google Scholar and various other social science and theology and religious studies online sites that can provide endless opportunities for research (one still needs a guide in many cases to help sort through the opportunities to locate the gold, if you will). Moreover, the seminary's resources include human capital such as the faculty and staff and fellow students.

One of the greatest resources to look for, however, is not even on the seminary campus. That is the resource of being connected to local churches. It is *the* resource link to evaluate as you consider various schools. For many of our pastoral training sites, the seminary will be in the local church. I know of some Anglican seminaries, for instance, where the seminary is in the cathedral campus. At any case, there should be strategic and synergistic relationships between local churches and the seminary. In the local church you will get the spiritual and practical resources you and your family need. In the local church you will get field opportunities. In the local church you can observe sessions, vestries, councils and the like in action. In the local church, you will worship and work with those men and women, the laity, who will one day call you and who will, during your seminary days, help you keep your theological training in perspective.

RESIDENCY-INTERNSHIP

It is important to recognize that theological education, following, as we have said previously, in the tradition of rabbinical training, is comprised—somewhat like medical training—of both an open academic component and the residential component. Oftentimes graduates out in the field for five years or so will receive a questionnaire about their experience in seminary. They will be asked to rate the seminary's effectiveness in matters such as administration, supervision of other clergy, relationship with adjudicatory, and other related practical issues. Invariably the graduate will respond that he did not receive proper training from the seminary. I quite understand his response and the consequential wringing of hands of seminary administrators. It appears that the seminary is forever on a quest to try to become more practical. At the same time the seminary can never quite get a handle on it. It is always an elusive target. I believe the challenge is a failure to appreciate the two components by the accrediting agency and quite possibly the seminary itself (if not, also, the graduate). Seminaries, like medical schools, are well-equipped to handle the academic work of teaching 'the anatomy' of the subject of pastoral ministry, but poorly equipped to teach the 'poetry' of the subject. The working laboratory of a local church or hospital is, on the other hand, well suited and usually eager to assume the responsibilities of teaching pastoral ministry in a real-life setting, i.e. residency.

Residency can (and should) happen in the first church where you are called after seminary. A residential program should be a formalized arrangement that involves the minister, his family, a supervisor, a peer—another minister who has been out of seminary for around five years, who has worked through some of the transitional issues—and a lay leader in the church. There should also be readings, videos, webinars, and live instructor-based interaction to process the twelve themes of that residential year (themes that are built upon calling, character, and competencies). The minister should cycle through each month with study, practice in the parish (visitation, preaching, etc.), writing a verbatim report, and meeting in theological self-reflection of how faith and seminary training integrated with *praxis*. These reflection meetings would occur with the supervisor (an older minister, at least fifteen years in the ministry), a peer, a lay leader (to give the perspective of the Church), and his wife (and, if they are old enough, even the new pastor's children).

It is our recommendation, then, to find that seminary, Bible college, pastoral training center, or other similar ministry of preparation that recognizes this two-component approach to pastoral training and has entered into such an arrangement. Such arrangements exist in the Western nations as well as in developing Christian churches in the global South and the global East and even in underground churches. My work in global theological education commissions has allowed me to see the work of theological higher education in this very area, even in the underground church, and I've been amazed at the way the church adapts in order to train her ministers through academics and residency. If you are reading this and seminary is already behind you and you didn't have that experience, you know the truth: that your first pastorate became de facto your residency. It cannot be avoided, can it?

HOW ABOUT DISTANCE LEARNING?

One of the great positive innovations in theological education has been the ability to integrate distance-learning models into the church's preparation of her pastors. The process is not without its critics, including myself at times, of its limitations, its trials and errors, its fits and starts, and its setbacks. However, we've come to a day where there is much to commend distance education in the preparation of pastors, missionaries, educators, and other Christian workers.

Some of the criticisms in the past have been aimed at the matter of a lack of interaction with the professor. Now, however, with both synchronous and asynchronous learning available, students, possibly, have more opportunity to interact with their professor than ever before. In my own experience I have found great joy with interaction with students in online classes. This is not to say it can replace face-to-face interaction. Even there we have found that there is a way around that with the establishment of study centers to go along with distance education or to offer intensive residential times along with distance education to create a sort of hybrid model.

Another past—and, quite honestly, continuing— criticism is that the online experience lacks the peer-to-peer spiritual, character, and vocational formation that we often refer to as the 'iron-sharpening-iron factor.' I have in past days been among those critics. Yet we hold that while pedagogical method is not devoid of theological value it is most often a neutral tool that can be shaped for good. It is easier to disparage the online or distance learning model if one has not engaged in it. I would urge my fellow critical clerics to take a *really solid* online course. With the advent of synchronous classes, discussion groups, small group rooms during classroom time (and then re-grouping to discuss the lesson) much has changed for the better. Learning experiences can include live, synchronous environments. Many professors construct such classes having prepared for the live class with asynchronous readings, discussion questions posted online on a virtual wall, weekly quizzes, and weekly research papers. Indeed, students often find the online experience even *more* engaging. As both a learner (in a graduate program at the University of North Carolina at Chapel Hill, a well-respected public, research university in America) and a professor (at two seminaries and one college), I know that I have benefited from the newer technologies in the delivery of quality theological education. Are all online courses the same? Of course not. Are all learning platforms equal? No. But there are good models out there. My guidance to the prospective seminary student today is to inspect the opportunities for both types of offerings in the seminaries you are considering: residential and online. Ask questions and do your research and pay close attention to the learning platforms and to synchronous and asynchronous learning commitments that the school has made.

There are many memories that I cherish from my own residential seminary days. One of them was when the students were able to go out after a particularly grueling class on, say, the Counter-Reformation, and eat a 'bottomless' bowl of soup and endless baskets of breadsticks all the while 'chewing' on the professor's insights about the founding of the Jesuits or the influence of the Counter-Reformation on Reformed missions (was it the deep content of our discussion or the bottomless soup bowls that I cherished—you decide!). I've often used this as an example of the sort of seminary student fellowship that simply could not be replicated online. However, recently my example was put to test when a group of students announced there would be a special fellowship hour—students only—following one of our classes to 'discuss' the professors' lectures and get to know each other. They were jokingly instructed to bring their own refreshments!

I believe that we have seen the budding of technology as well as the maturity of a corresponding pedagogy. These have become new 'Roman roads' for delivering the gospel and preparing the gospel messenger in our day. Let us pray that we would use these roadways wisely for the kingdom of God.

WHY YOU SHOULD CONSIDER A MOVE TO A SEMINARY CAMPUS

The Power of Leaving and Following

Despite the temptation to follow a distance learning approach, which is so popular and so available today, I would urge many of you to consider the dynamics of actually leaving to follow your call.

A minister of the gospel is always called to go. We are called to 'go and make disciples.' For most of us, this means that we will not minister in our hometowns. Even our Lord said, 'A prophet is without honor in his own country.' Most ministers will serve several churches in addition to other sorts of ecclesiastical appointments. Most of those will require a move. Abraham moved. Moses moved. Jeremiah moved. Amos moved. Paul moved. Leaving to follow Christ in order to carry the gospel to others generally requires moving. Now, it's not as bad as it was for some of our brothers in years past—like Methodist pastors, who would move every two years or so—but it's still part and parcel of the job.

So, what am I getting at here? To leave and follow Christ in a ministry of preparation (the essence of seminary) is, for most of us, our first act of total submission to the gospel call.

Whether it's across the state or across the nation (or globe, if you are so inclined), following the Lord and moving to the campus of the seminary is still an exercise in ministerial faithfulness.

THE CENTRIFUGAL EFFECT OF A MENTOR

Another great reason why one should go to seminary rather than experience it through the Internet is to get hold of the centrifugal effect of a good mentor. Let me explain.

Seminary professors differ from other professors. They are, almost universally, ordained ministers themselves. Most will have had considerable years of parish work behind them. All of them at your choice of seminaries, I trust, will have been personally called by God to equip the church by training her pastors. The vision of 2 Timothy 2:2 is burnished into the souls of most of them:

> *and the things that you have heard from me among many witnesses, commit these to faithful men who will be able to teach others also (2 Tim. 2:2).*

The seminary professor is a mentor who instills vision into his students. Seminary is all about imparting a vision of God, of man, of Christ, of the church, and of the power of the gospel. We may apply the words of Joel's prophecy to the fruit of a good seminary professor's labor: '…Your old men shall dream dreams, Your young men shall see visions' (Joel 2:28).

Seminary should provide mentors who are like space rockets; they propel future ministers off into the unreached worlds with such a strong vision of God and His plan that the vision—their rocket booster—will keep them moving forward for the rest of their lives.

The booster will fall away, but the ship will go through the initial difficult atmospheric years of early ministry, through the unexpected trials of parish work and to a faithful completion of one's mission, based on the influence of the booster on their initial speed and trajectory.

That is why you must consider leaving for seminary. You simply need the boost.

THE BENEFIT OF IRON SHARPENING IRON

Obviously, one of the main differences between doing seminary work online and in the classroom is interaction with others. You need interaction, not only with teachers, but equally as important, with fellow students.

> *As iron sharpens iron, So a man sharpens the countenance of his friend (Prov. 27:17).*

God calls all kinds of people into ministry, and each of you may be different in your make-up. But if God has called you to preach, then you are all mined out of the same cavern. Iron needs iron, says the Word of God. This is yet another reason that in-person, joint study can benefit both you and others.

Most people arrive at seminary with preconceived notions, expectations, and fears. And after a few days or weeks, the reality of seminary sets in—both the aspects that are better than you expected, and the difficulties that mar your romanticized view of what would occur there. These are the times when fellowship with others who are encountering the same experiences can be helpful. And, this is an opportunity for you to contribute to the building up of Christ's body as well. This cannot be accomplished in the same way when you are simply emailing assigned work or even dialoging in writing on a topic. In-person study brings with it a very different dynamic and opportunity.

THE BENEFIT TO THE FAMILY

For seminarians who already have a spouse and perhaps even children, the physical move to a seminary can be, in the best cases, stressful, and in the worse cases, crushing. At the same time, though, the move to seminary is the pivotal event in family life that transforms a family into a pastoral family. A man can be an attorney and his wife may be only minimally involved with his day-to-day career. A person may be a sheet metal worker and his spouse be very distant from his work, but not so in the ministry. The wife and the children are intimately involved with the work of the minister of the gospel, and the sooner one learns that, the better. Leaving to go to seminary is helpful in this regard.

Seminary is something that you will face together, even if you are the only one formally enrolled in school.

Again, for a healthy family, the transition out of your former life and into seminary is recommended and is very helpful in the process of surrendering to God's call.

In our family, we tried to move to seminary once, and God stopped it. He stopped it because our daughter was not ready for it. She had some deep spiritual issues that had to be dealt with prior to our family going into the ministry. Did we know it at the time? Not completely, though we had an idea. We were disappointed at first, but God showed her the problem, and there was significant healing. Once this was taken care of, the Lord cleared a path for us the following year.

If there are underlying spiritual issues that need addressing and that are not being dealt with in your family, ask God to show them to you and to bring healing before making any move. It is a good idea to solicit the observation of others who love you and who can help you come to terms with this vital subject.

THE BENEFIT TO YOUR FUTURE CHURCHES

Personally, I knew that I could never stand before a congregation and admonish them to step out in faith in God if I did not step out in faith to go to seminary. That conviction proved to be a good one. God met my needs along the way and taught me truths there that I could have never learned had I taken the safer route of staying at my home. The church benefits, then, when her ministers have experienced the power of God firsthand. A minister who has left all to follow God, first at seminary, and later for a pastoral call, is a minister who has a story to tell about God's faithfulness. Show me such a minister and I will show you a congregation that is grateful that its minister left all else to follow his call.

6
The Life of a Seminary Family

I will never forget our lives at seminary. Was it hectic? Unmercifully. Was it fatiguing? Most certainly. Would I do it again? Without a doubt, I would. My wife and I can honestly say that our seminary years were some of the very best in our family life.

Contrary to some popularly held notions, seminary is not designed to break you, discourage you, or take your faith away from you! Seminary is a formation station. It should be a meaningful time for each member of the family, and I firmly believe that it can be.

GETTING THERE
When we went to seminary, our family consisted of my wife, myself, our daughter (who was in high school at the time), and my ninety-one-year-old aunt (who had reared me).

I will never forget that move. My wife and daughter went first and moved in with the Dean of Faculty and his wife. Two weeks after I packed up our home and made the 1,500-mile trip. My aunt remained behind at a nursing home until we could get settled. About three weeks after I arrived, my wife flew back to get my aunt, and the two of them returned together.

Now, prior to our move, my wife and I had made a trip down to the seminary (which was in Fort Lauderdale). We secured a real estate representative who was recommended by the seminary. My wife told him our needs, and our budget, and the three of us spent a few days looking around (and even praying together about it). We found a perfect home for our needs.

I would definitely recommend taking that scouting trip to set up employment, housing, schooling, and to get a general feel for what will become your home for three to five years. This is also a good time to talk about how your lives will be different during the seminary years and to get on the same page regarding division of labor, family routines, and other expectations for the seminary years.

SETTLING IN

One of the most important steps in making a transition is to immediately find your place. By that I mean that each member of the family must begin to fit in to the new locale. This must be intentional. Someone is going to have to make it happen. If you are a parent, you should assist your children in thinking through how this will happen for them specifically. If you are married, you should think about not only your own but also your spouse's needs in this area.

The circumstances themselves may be of help here. Seminary, work, school, church life, and ordinary household chores and errands will begin to drive you toward settling in. For many seminarians today, this process will not be unlike one of your transfers or a permanent change of duty station in the military. If you resist the process and give in to thinking about what could have been had you stayed in your career, you are on a sure pathway for unhappiness.

> *Trust in the LORD with all your heart,*
> *And lean not on your own understanding;*
> *In all your ways acknowledge Him,*
> *And He shall direct your paths (Prov. 3:5,6).*

You need to settle in.

ROLES

Before we went to seminary, I took great pride in my lawn and spent no small amount of time in cultivating it. With the advent of term papers, sermons to write, visits to make, and reading assignments totaling two thousand pages a week, my ability to even mow the lawn was seriously impaired! So, my wife, who formerly was only the proprietor of the house, became quite adept at gardening. In fact, her running battle with the hedges in our south Florida rental became the stuff of family folklore. I even bought her an electric hedge trimmer for her birthday!

All of this to say that at seminary, because of school and work and ministry training, old schedules, habits, and roles must be flexible. Now that seminary is well behind me (and post-graduate school after that), I am happy to say that I run the weed-eater once more, but during seminary, there were necessary role exchanges for the sake of the Gospel.

Talk it out now and be ready, at least temporarily, to adjust your roles to meet the mission. Even though you have already discussed some of these changes before making the trip, there is no way to anticipate every change or every new circumstance. Schedule times to revisit your plans, and work on good communication so that one person does not become resentful or frustrated when certain tasks inevitably 'fall through the cracks.' These years can be an excellent opportunity to improve in the area of teamwork.

CHILDREN

We left for seminary with an eleventh grader. We were, thus, understandably concerned about the move. But as it turned out, God took care of our concerns and our daughter. She flourished during those seminary years and even met her future husband while there.

God sent His own Son into a family and thus blessed that most basic of His human building instruments. We need to, throughout the process of call and response, affirm that institution and affirm the heritage of the Lord: our children.

I remember talking to the daughter of a restaurant owner who told me that running a restaurant is definitely a team sport! There were always dishes to wash, floors to clean, supplies to order, food to cook, and customers to wait on. The same is true of the ministry. It's a team sport, and the team is the family. Seminary is a ministry of preparation; therefore, going to seminary and giving the children an opportunity to make the schedule work are important. What they learn during that time will help them to transition, as you must, into the joys and challenges of parish life.

While you might help your children understand their responsibilities in the new location, don't let them stop being children! Be sure to plan some down-time and relaxation together as a family.

I once saw a little fellow on the playground who was the son of the Episcopal rector. I said to this little five-year-old who was playing with my own son, 'Aren't you the Episcopal minister's son?' 'No,' he answered sharply, 'I am my Daddy's son!'

Yes, that is it. They are first and foremost children who need all that other children need.

Furthermore, do not stop being a parent to them. Don't let seminary studies and the pursuit of a ministerial career spoil your children's childhood. If you fail at being a parent, you are washed up as a minister before you even start. God desires the hearts of the fathers to be turned to the children.[1] Encourage them in their own pursuits. Prioritize them. Be there for them. Involve them in your ministry, but don't put them on parade. Don't fall into the temptation of trying to create an image of the perfect pastoral family. It works for a while, but then it can get ugly when they get old enough to sense what's going on. Just be a parent. Let them just be children.

---

1   Malachi 4:4-6 and Luke 1:17.

FINANCES

When we went off to school, I sold stocks, depleted savings, appealed to my home church for support, worked full-time and went to school full-time, and even pulled off an internship that had a small stipend.

I needed every last penny of it. Seminary costs, and so does raising a family. It's great to pay off all of your bills before you go. If you can do that, fine. If your financial obligation has prevented you from going to seminary, then wrest yourself free. Your testimony is at stake. If, however, you have a reasonable debt, but want to wait until everything is perfect, I say to you, 'Let the dead bury the dead.' It might be that those finances and your desire to have everything just so have become an instrument of the enemy, to prevent you from being obedient. Like most of us, you probably will have to work and go to school at the same time. Actually, the combination can teach you a great deal about time management, so it's not all bad—though certainly challenging!

Obviously, if you are not budgeting, the time to start is now. You will need a financial system in order to get through. Remember to budget some time (and money) to get away for a family vacation and for weekly retreats for you and your spouse, if you are married. For Mae and me, this meant a Saturday afternoon stroll in a suburban shopping mall and a couple of coffees. This activity cost us about three dollars per week, but the memories and the investment in the marriage remain priceless.

Since I am arguing for seminary as a ministry in itself—a ministry of preparation, a mission if there ever was one—I believe one of the best preliminary things you can do is to raise support for your ministry. Hopefully, your local church has encouraged you to do this and will want to stand with you during this time. However, this is another reason why good budgeting is important. In order to encourage accountability, you should know where your money is coming from, how much you have, and where you are spending it. This will help you assess when you need to ask for more and how that money will be used once you receive it.

FRIENDS AND FELLOWSHIP

Seminary was one of the greatest experiences in our lives and most certainly in our marriage. Perhaps a primary reason that we feel that way is that we made and have retained deep friendships. Think about it: You all are there in the same place, have gone through the same experience of following a call, and are desperately trying to memorize Hebrew verb forms! You can't have more in common than that!

If you are thinking that training for ministry means launching out without friends, forget it. God will provide you with deep, lasting friendships built upon a love for the gospel and a common call to labor in His fields. This is all the more important because the friends you make in seminary are people you can turn to throughout the rest of your ministry, whether you stay in one place for years or move quite a bit. These people will understand you in different ways to the friends you make in future ministry.

SPIRITUAL FORMATION

As our society transitioned from an agrarian-based society to an industrial society and then again, in our own day, to an information-based society, we have had to make adjustments. Modernity hasn't always been kind to the soul. Churches have had to be intentional about ministries in light of the modern challenges we face.

There is a similar threat to the man and woman and family as they go into seminary. The demands of school, work, and family chores work together to potentially threaten our spirituality. Amazing as it may seem, seminarians are more prone to spiritual dryness, and even decay, than the average committed Christian.

Why is this the case? In short, seminary poses a threat to balance. It will become possible for you to study the doctrine of the Holy Spirit and yet quench His power in your own life. How? By approaching the doctrine in a dry, academic, detached fashion. The motivation for your understanding of the Holy Spirit as He is revealed in Scripture is singular: to pass the upcoming examination. This is, of course, necessary. But far more important is your motivation to grow in grace as well as in knowledge. The overriding motivation in your life remains: follow Christ in the power of the Spirit.

It is true, also, that seminary life is similar to pastoral life. Those who handle holy things day in and day out are prone to treat their spiritual lives with an equally perfunctory spirit.

How do you avoid this trap of the ministry? In a phrase, the answer is this: Go to the mountain.

The Lord's greatest work seemed to be carried on before and after ministry on a mountain. Consider some of these passages:

> *Now after six days Jesus took Peter, James, and John his brother, led them up on a high mountain by themselves (Matt. 17:1).*

> *Then the eleven disciples went away into Galilee, to the mountain which Jesus had appointed for them (Matt. 28:16).*

> *Now it came to pass in those days that He went out to the mountain to pray, and continued all night in prayer to God (Luke 6:12).*

The mountain is the place where God is. The mountain in your life, seminarian or minister, is the place where others aren't looking, where professors aren't examining, where parishioners and peers are absent. It is the place where you and God meet and carry on your soul's unseen business. What happens there will affect everything else in your life and, consequently, your ministry.

Make daily and weekly appointments, then, to meet God on the mountain, or in the closet (Matt. 6:6), and explore your life with Him. Ask Him to show you His glory in your life and your work. Plead with Christ to examine the sinful motivations, sinful propensities, and sinful acts in your life. Ask the Lord to forgive you, to cleanse you, to renew you. Lift up others, especially those who trouble you in your life.[2]

Do this, and the mountain will transform the daily valley into a sanctuary.

---

2   'But I say to you, love your enemies, bless those who curse you, do good to those who hate you, and pray for those who spitefully use you and persecute you' (Matt. 5:44).

7
The Ministry of a Seminarian

There are some seminarians who mistakenly believe that once their degree is in hand, they will somehow mystically be transformed into a minister. The reality is that your call should transform you and that seminary is actually your first duty station as a minister. Your deportment in your classes and in your relationship to your fellow students, faculty, and administration will forge a pattern for future ministry assignments. The seminarian has a ministry. What is it?

A SEMINARIAN'S SCRIPTURE

But you, man of God, flee from all this, and pursue righteousness, godliness, faith, love, endurance and gentleness. Fight the good fight of the faith. Take hold of the eternal life to which you were called when you made your good confession in the presence of many witnesses (1 Tim. 6:11-12, NIV).

The ministry of preparation can be like training camp in the National Football League: players are cut because they succumbed to outside interests rather than concentrating on the things that make for good football players.

So, too, as you are gathered for your studies, there are dangers. Some of you can't wait to get going in seminary, but your minds have not grasped the reality that you are now entering the ministry. Some of you imagine that you will go through seminary, and then, after ordination, some sort of magic dust will be sprinkled on you and you can begin to act like a minister.

I believe that young Timothy was, in essence, a seminarian under the professorship of Paul. What Paul says to Timothy in 1 Timothy 6:3-10 is an outline of the way Timothy is to approach his ministry.

I want you to pause and, likewise, consider your ministry as a seminarian, using the charge given to Timothy.

YOUR MINISTRY IS TO BE A MAN OF GOD (1 TIM. 6:11)

The way Paul addresses Timothy is important. This is a title of honor, of nobility, of character. A man selected for the ministry must, first and foremost, be a man of God. So as one pursues the studies required to practice as a 'doctor of souls,' it is required that such a one, first, attend to his own soul. Then, he must be about the cure of souls in his own home. It is only then that he can apply the medicine of Word, Sacrament, and Prayer to the spirits of others. So how shall you then be that man of God?

YOU WILL BE A MAN OF GOD AS YOU MAKE GOD YOUR FIRST PRIORITY.

This should happen every day, but also in larger patterns over the weeks, months, and years of seminary study. For instance, I would advocate serving the Lord and refraining from your studies on His day. Tithe your money and your time to Christ. God needs neither, but you need to prioritize the Lord. Be a man of God.

YOU WILL BE A MAN OF GOD AS YOU SEEK PERSONAL HOLINESS. Ordination does not suddenly make you a man of God. You must show yourselves approved unto God *right now* and *over time.* Use seminary to practice holiness. All eyes are upon you as a model of what a man of God is to be. Be a man of God.

YOU WILL BE A MAN OF GOD AS YOU LOOK UPON YOUR STUDIES AS SACRED.

As a pastor, teacher, missionary, or whatever and however you serve, your chief business is always communicating the Word of God and providing God's answers to everyday problems. To do so, you must study. A man of God is a man who has sat at the feet of the Lord and supped with Him from His Word. Use your studies in languages, history, systematic preaching, and liturgics to honor God. Go into every class with the attitude that you are dedicating this to Him. Be a man of God.

Now, look at Paul's explosion of directives to young Timothy. These are God's words to you today.

YOUR MINISTRY IS TO TURN YOUR BACK ON THE WORLD

…flee these things… (1 Tim. 6:11)

Flee what things? First Timothy 6:3-10 tells us about error and greed in the world. Paul mentions pride, useless wrangling of men, philosophical disputes, and discontentment.

You, too, must turn your back on error and greed, which mark the occupations of so many others in the world.

TURN YOUR BACK ON PRIDE.

Pride will attack you in seminary. You may be tempted to be proud because you are in seminary and the rest of your Sunday school class is not. You may become a know-it-all and try to exhibit your newfound theological insights to others. I assure you that others easily discern such pride, and your display will be offensive and hurt your ministry.

I read an anonymous Puritan quote that is helpful to us at this point:

> When God intends to fill a soul, He first makes it empty; when He intends to enrich a soul, He first makes it poor; when He intends to exalt a soul, He first makes it sensible of its own miseries, wants, and nothingness.

There is nothing so odious as a seminarian filled with pride. It is grievous to those of us who lead you, and it hurts the church in general. Remember that Jesus said the greatest in the church is the one who serves. Use your theology to help others to drink from the deep wells of the Bible, not as a showy garment that draws attention to yourself.

TURN YOUR BACK ON USELESS WRANGLING AND PHILOSOPHICAL
DISPUTES.

I don't mean that you should not take up genuine theological issues at seminary. If there is one place where you should be allowed to do so, it is here. Iron sharpens iron, the Bible says, and so it must be at seminary.

No, what is prohibited is what the great ancient father, Chrysostom, described as:

> ... *poor wretches of sophists shouting and abusing each other, and their disciples, as they call them, squabbling, and many writers of books reading their stupid compositions, and many poets singing their poems, and many jugglers exhibiting their marvels, and many soothsayers giving their meaning of prodigies, and a thousand rhetoricians twisting lawsuits....*[1]

The picture is of philosophers putting on a show, craving praise and competing with each other for attention from the crowds.

Seminarians can be like that. Ministers can be like that. All show.

It is interesting for me to listen to the questions of many of my fellow elders when a young minister comes up for ordination examination. Often what comes out of their mouths is a display of the last thing they read or some specialized interest they have.

Interesting, too, is to listen to the comments of some seminarians in class. They are eager, like a peacock before a hen, to display their learning for the sake of drawing attention to their intellectual prowess. It should not be so.

---

1   As quoted in William Barclay, *The Daily Bible Study Series: The Letters to Timothy, Titus, and Philemon*, Revised Edition, '1 Timothy,' (Philadelphia: Westminster Press, 1975), 125.

Flee from this and pursue learning with righteousness and an eye towards pleasing God and building up the church.

TURN YOUR BACK ON DISCONTENTMENT.

This might sound like an unreasonable command. Yet it is one of those Gospel directives that must be put directly before one's own spirit. God who commands will give Gospel grace to fulfill it.

If you come to seminary right out of college, many of your college friends may also be in graduate school—business schools, law schools, medical schools, and the like. All of you are on a professional track that will lead to an important place in society. But you, seminarian, are in a different class: poor! The others are generally well financed with the potential for huge profits in the future.

Trying to go to seminary, work two jobs (with your spouse and kids also chipping in to make ends meet), juggle a schedule that fits everything in, and doing all of this with no promise of a huge monetary windfall in the future, can lead to discontentment.

If you face this particular temptation, only remember this: While others are learning about profit margins, court cases, and anatomical Latin, you, my friend, are pursuing God and the ministry of Jesus Christ. With all due respect and gratitude for the other professions, in the end, your work will greatly outlast any fruit they will have gathered in this life. You will baptize converts; catechize children; marry couples; console the grieving; and, week after week, proclaim the unsearchable riches of Jesus Christ, who is able to save souls!

Whenever you get discontented with the life of a seminarian, only consider the high and holy calling to which you aspire and the eternal life that you are gathering for yourself and those who are touched by your ministry.

CONCLUSION

In conclusion, your ministry is first and foremost, to be a man of God and, in doing so, to turn your back on the world. How do you do that? Paul gives the answer:

> ...*Pursue righteousness, godliness, faith, love, endurance and gentleness. Fight the good fight of the faith. Take hold of the eternal life to which you were called... (1 Tim. 6:11, 12).*

In other words, be actively engaged with becoming more like Christ.

I will never forget when I sat where you are now sitting. I had worked and planned and dreamed of seminary for a long time. Finally, at last, I found myself sitting in the Orientation Chapel. My mind was spinning with thoughts of studying theology under my well-grounded and all-wise professors. I was a bit heady about it all and just a little proud of being there.

Then, Dr. Robert Reymond, who was the Professor of Systematic Theology at Knox Theological Seminary, addressed us in that chapel. He ended his message with words that reached out and grabbed my heart and stirred me to the depths of my sin-recovering soul:

> *Brothers, if you go through three to four years of seminary, attending all of the classes, reading all of the required texts, listening to all of the lectures, memorizing all of the charts and paradigms, passing all of the examinations, and are*

handed that sheepskin—yet you don't love Jesus more and know Him better at the end than at the beginning, then you have failed, and your time here will have been a waste.

If you are a seminarian, you are already in ministry. Flee from the world of error and greed and take upon yourself, even now, the mantle of humility and servanthood that marks every great minister of the gospel. Lay hold of the mind and character and perfect will of Almighty God who called you to the ministry. Amen.

8

Finding Your Place in the Church

—or, 'What color is your pulpit?'

For the message.
Prompt me, God;
But not yet.
When I spake,
Though it be you who speak
Through me, something is lost.
The meaning is in the waiting.
—George Herbert[1]

At this point in the book, I am assuming that God has called you to the ministry, that you, in fact, are possessed of both the inward and outward calls to the ordained gospel ministry. You are either on your way to seminary, just graduating seminary, just leaving seminary, or perhaps, are reading this as you are well into your vocation. Assuming that, I want to discuss a topic that leads not a few ordained ministers to a place of near despair: now what?

---

1   Herbert, George, and Helen Wilcox, 'The Glance (86).' In *100 Poems* (Cambridge: Cambridge University Press, 2016), 138.

What Color is Your Parachute? is the title of a popular guide to helping individuals match their gifts and dreams to the suitable career.[2] This chapter is similarly concerned with discussing and, hopefully, assisting you in the process of matching your gifts and dreams to the suitable need within the ministry. The vision of this chapter (indeed, this book) is to strengthen you and in some way stir you on to a good landing in the ordained ministry.

The ministry is not, of course, about self-actualization and self-fulfillment (the apparent overarching interest of many career help books). Jesus came to serve, and we are no better than our Master. Rather, the ministry is God's answer to the spiritual needs of the world. Men and women are saved; sanctified; taught; fed and clothed; put in their right minds, so to speak; and called to a better way through the instrumentality of the ordained ministry. 'What color is your pulpit?' then, should be a question to those who are intent on giving their lives away to God and to others. This is decidedly not an appeal to only your self-fulfillment, but to help you consider God's best place for you within the ministry.

Though I have sub-titled this 'What Color Is Your Pulpit?' I don't mean to imply that every ministry involves a pulpit ministry in a local church. I do, though, mean to say that every area of ministry, every grouping and subset of the ordained task is and must be in some way living out

2   Richard Nelson Bolles, *What Color Is Your Parachute?* 2000 Edition: A Practical Manual for Job-Hunters & Career-Changers, 30th Rev. edition (Berkeley, California: Ten Speed Press, 1999).

the ministry of the Word. When I say 'pulpit,' then, I am referring here to the task of preaching and administering the Sacraments or Ordinances of the church of Jesus Christ. I am saying that if we are ministers of the gospel, we are all, at our most basic job description, just preachers.

I have served as the Chairman of the Candidates and Credentials Committee of a regional judicatory in my own denomination (The Presbyterian Church in America). One of my jobs when I am in this role, along with my fellow presbyters, is to examine ministers and their calls to see whether the work to which they are being called is met with the goals of ordination.

There was once a man that came to us who described the work to which he was called. This fellow, who had been working at this position for some time, described his leadership of this particular foreign mission. It all sounded very good and was a profitable and worthy ministry. The question that our committee had, though, was whether or not he needed to be ordained in order to do the ministry. Ministers are called to be God's agents of Word and Sacrament. There are many ways that Word and Sacrament works its way out in various agencies of the church and of respective missions (and we will consider some of them here). There are also outstanding ministries and positions within those ministries that do not require Word and Sacrament to reach their stated goals. Several of us determined that in this fellow's case, he did not need ordination credentials to carry out the functions of that job.

Every ministry must have a pulpit. Every ministry in the church that requires an ordained minister of the gospel to fill it has a place for Word and Sacrament, in some tangible fashion.

The look and feel of the pulpit changes as one observes the various roles in the church. The senior pastor of a multi-staff church is different from the solo pastorate in some ways. The assistant minister for youth has different goals and requires distinctly different gifts and even personality than a church planter for Eastern Europe. The itinerant evangelist, the seminary professor, the college campus chaplain, the military chaplain are all different (and all alike, in that they are all ministries of Word and Sacrament).

Where do you fit in?

HOW DO YOU KNOW?

If I didn't believe that God would show you where He wants you, I would do better not to write this chapter or this book. But, I do believe that the Lord Himself will show you His will for you. Did Christ not tell us to 'Ask, and it will be given to you; seek, and you will find; knock, and it will be opened to you'? (Matt. 7:7)

Begin, then, with earnest prayer in this regard. He called you. He will be faithful to guide you. As He led you to surrender to His call to preach the gospel, He will likewise make Himself known to you in this area.

In this matter of which ministry is the best one for me, I would like to offer a few simple indicators or signposts that will guide you in your journey. Romans 12:3-8 provides a fine paradigm for considering which ministry is for you. In that passage, Paul, after calling the Romans to transformed living in this world, reminds them that they will live this out in different ways:

> *For as we have many members in one body, but all the members do not have the same function ... having then gifts differing according to the grace that is given to us... (Rom. 12:4-6).*

The first signpost along the way is most assuredly in your heart right now or is being formed within you. What is it? Passion. Paul talks about a different grace given to each of us by God. Grace is the operative key to our salvation and also to our ministry. Grace is given us at the point of our need, and when we receive that grace at that need, we are healed—we are saved.

God will give you a passion for something, for someone, for some need, arising out of that grace in your own life. This is the first great indicator. Show me a recovered alcoholic that God has called to preach, and I will show you a great candidate to minister to alcoholics. Of course, there are many fine ministers in that capacity who never had to fight that battle. I would submit, though, that when God touches your life in one particular area, He gives you a passion for others who are still in the sin and misery from which you were delivered. So, I would say, just go to the Lord and see what He has done in your life, and go from there.

So, passion is the first signpost, and I would submit that giftedness is the second. The apostle Paul mentions prophecy, service, teaching, exhorting, giving, leading, and mercy. I don't believe that this is intended as the exhaustive list of New Testament gifts but rather is an example of the variety of God-given gifts. Now, if you have a passion and a gift that are compatible—and there is a need and an outward calling—then there is probably a divine match. Of course, if your passion is seeing youth discipled, but you and others assess you as lacking fundamental qualities that endear you to teenagers, you obviously don't have a match. Therefore, passion and giftedness must be linked.

Perhaps a word should be said, as well, about measuring instruments. There are a variety of psychological tests, personality inventories, and personal gift inventories that are available to help you in this. I am not in the least opposed to these as a matter of principle. I think the Myers-Briggs® and the DISC® temperament profiles are quite helpful. But, when I have taken these tests (and I have taken them before, during and after seminary training), I have found that they usually change little and tell me what I generally already know (not that affirmation is not needed—it is, and I commend these instruments to you).

I urge anyone wanting to know 'what color is my pulpit' to begin with a recollection of the grace of God in your life, the passion and faith which God gave you, and your gifts and interests which you and others see in you.

THE VARIETIES OF MINISTRIES CONSIDERED
In an effort to help you, I want to address several traditional ministry positions and describe what I think are the passions, gifts, and interests peculiar to each one. Unless

otherwise noted, each position is assumed to be a home ministry—that is, not a foreign missionary experience. Of course, there will be situations with different features than these. But I offer these as a general guideline or starting point for your own assessment of yourself or of a particular ministry context.

SOLO PASTOR

The solo pastor is what most people think about when they think about the ministry. There is variety even within this particular ministry (and within all of the other jobs I will list). There are solo pastors in rural churches, new churches, churches in need of revitalization, and urban churches. Each of these respective positions demands a peculiar mix of passions and gifts. I want to concentrate on the common denominator issues of the solo pastor, no matter where that may exist.

I once read an essay in which the writer reminisced about his childhood pastor. He wrote that everything he knew about theology and church and servanthood had its origin in that godly man who dressed in khakis every day except Sunday; he could be seen during the week sometimes walking through the small community hospital, sometimes cutting the grass at church, sometimes knocking down dirt dauber nests out of the corner of the sanctuary with a broom handle, and always ready to tell you about Jesus Christ.

That is not a bad thumbnail sketch of the solo pastor.

Passions: The solo pastor is usually a minister who likes serving in smaller churches, less administration, less leadership of staff, and more hands-on ministry. Indeed, the solo pastor has a passion for equipping the saints for the work of ministry in a real one-on-one fashion. The person cut out for this position should be one who, perhaps, finds as much or more satisfaction in leading a workday at the church as in leading an evangelistic campaign for a major city. To the solo pastor, there is no greater joy than in shepherding the flock through one-on-one visitation at their homes, in their places of employment, or at the graduation ceremony.

Warnings: High-energy drivers who prefer more expansive ministry fields may find the solo pastorate confining. Yet, it may be you need to discover the joy and contentment of a solo pastorate, even if you prefer a multi-staff church, or a church plant, or a mission agency.

Alternatively, if you see your calling as primarily a shepherd, not one who delegates the caring to other shepherds—i.e., a shepherd to shepherds—then the solo pastorate would be the goal. There are few more vocationally satisfying roles than that of the parish vicar.

MULTI-STAFF SENIOR PASTOR

The senior pastor of a church is essentially the minister responsible for the equipping and shepherding work of the congregation, who, because of the size of the congregation or the level of competency and/or efficiency expected by church leadership, leads a staff of ordained and non-ordained people to carry out the pastoral charge. Thus, the senior pastor delegates respective components of the ministerial task to people with matching competencies (youth pastor, visitation pastor, Christian education pastor, etc.).

Passions: This ministerial profile calls for an individual who is generally a leader (leaders like to lead and usually seek out positions that are not lived out in greater isolation, such as a solo pastorate), and who sees things in terms of the big picture. The senior pastor position may be seen as an executive position, but in truth, those who lead like that are prone to get into trouble in one way or another. The senior pastor is best seen as the senior servant. His job is still to equip the saints for the work of ministry; it is just that this is accomplished with more than one person.

Warnings: Some are prone to idealize this position. Some see the job as higher up the ladder than perhaps a solo pastor. The best senior pastors will quickly tell you that there is nothing glamorous about bearing the burden of either a large congregation or a congregation with high expectations. Moreover, the senior pastor's roles as fellow minister and yet supervisor to other ministers is a tricky one that has few counterparts in the business world. In order to succeed, the senior pastor spends or should spend a great deal of time in prayer, in encouraging and praying with and for his staff, and in preparing to lead the big groups (i.e., the worship services, boards) of the church, rather than the smaller groups (i.e., Sunday school, Bible studies).

MULTI-STAFF ASSOCIATE PASTOR

Following on the back of the senior pastor is our consideration of his specialty ministers. The ministers of youth, Christian education, visitation, and the like fulfill the overall pastoral charge in such a church.

Passions: One primary passion must be for the specialty itself, whatever that might be. You see yourself as working in a team environment, encouraging others, and looking to other peers for your encouragement. You are more comfortable in smaller group settings, in fulfilling the mandates rather than setting them. Of primary importance, in my opinion, is the personal trait of what the Bible calls 'helpers.' You are a supporter rather than the up-front leader.

Warnings: This is not a place to hide out. Some try to hide out in the specialties because they are not fond of any sort of leadership. All ministers are leaders of God's people. The staff minister is responsible for leading in his particular department. Similarly, some might think this is a good place to hide from the harder work of either a solo pastor or senior pastor. Again, this is patently wrong. I have known staff ministers to actually spend more time working at their position than senior pastors. The highly specialized nature of the ministry seems to encourage people to think that you have nothing else to do but serve them. As a result, departmental ministry can often bear the burden of doing your primary ministry task, plus filling in for the senior pastor when he is out and, in mega-churches, covering other departments during vacation season or when there is a vacancy. This, like all ministries, is hard work—or should be. There is much work in the harvest fields of our Lord. Ministers are called to realize this and embrace it, not hide from it or whine about it.

CHURCH-PLANTER

All ministries that you see up and running were once just a man and a vision. At some point, that church you attend, that seminary you are going to, or that hospital you are recovering in was the heartbeat of an entrepreneurial spirit who saw God's kingdom and human need and said to himself, 'This cannot be. God is too great and the condition here too bad. Who will go and build? Who has seen God's plan and will dare stand in the gap of this age and announce that plan? *I* must.'

This is the soul of the church planter. Now, when I say church planter, I would include all of those more apostolic souls who work outside of the settled ministries of the church. They may be planting churches or schools or nursing homes or television and radio ministries, but the common denominator is their resolve to change the way things are by creating a new extension of God's kingdom for the need. Often, church planters end up as solo pastors, senior pastors, parachurch ministry leaders, and even itinerant evangelists.

Passions: A great deal has been written about church planters in our day. The study of the assessment and sending of church planters has become quite scientific. I would recommend that those of you interested in further exploration of that ministry take advantage of the several good publications out on the subject. For my purposes here, let me just say that the ministry of a church planter always begins with one who feels things deeply. The church planter looks across a community, sees a need, and feels that need himself. He goes to God and believes that God is telling him to go and meet the need. He hears the cry of the oppressed—be they suburbanites drowning in a meaningless neighborhood of materialism or inner city families being torn apart at the heart by drugs, gang violence, and hopelessness. When the church planter senses the will of God in these matters, it leads him to do something. By nature, then, the church planter is a risk taker. The church planter does not ask, 'What will be the salary?' The church planter is consumed by the vision of the ministry itself and will build the infrastructure to support any salary or no salary. Like Paul (the model for all such ministers), the church planter will mend tents to fulfill his calling. Another necessary trait of all such ministers is the God-given gift to articulate their vision in such a way that others begin to see the vision and gather around it. Churches are planted, not because Mr. and Mrs. Jones liked the nursery facilities and so joined Pastor Steve's church—because there *is* no nursery and there *are* no facilities! Instead, Mr. and Mrs. Jones joined the church because when Pastor Steve casts his vision of God and His kingdom, Mr. and Mrs. Jones, maybe for the first time in their lives, could see what was not there and believe, somehow, that it would happen. This is the gift of the church planter—really, the gift of faith.

Warnings: The one who sees himself as a church planter can, without controlling insight and wisdom, also see himself as a nonconformist, a real maverick; or he often, through the process of casting vision and leading the charge for following the vision, can become a maverick. God did not call us to be lone wolves or loose cannons. Paul's ministry, though given to him by Christ personally, started officially when Barnabas brought the new preacher to the church officials (Acts 9:27).[3] Even the great church planter of Tarsus recognized the divine limitations and parameters placed over individual ministers. When a conflict arose in the early church over the issue of grace, Paul appealed to the larger church at Jerusalem to settle the matter. The Lord has not made lone wolves, but relational creatures, and has put us in a pack; it's called the church. We also don't just fire at random but aim our cannons in harmony with each other. We are the army of the Lord, not guerilla mercenaries. Submission and servanthood are watchwords for all of us. The church planter must recognize that the very same passion and giftedness that propels him onto the field to meet the need and to gather others around who will see his vision, can get him into trouble. I have known several church planters who forfeited their ministries because of a failure to either see this trait or to guard against it. Conversely, some might see this ministry as attractive without coming to terms with the tremendous physical and emotional energy that is expended. Moreover, this ministry, perhaps

---

3   'But Barnabas took him and brought him to the apostles. And he declared to them how he had seen the Lord on the road, and that He had spoken to him, and how he had preached boldly at Damascus in the name of Jesus.' (Acts 9:27).

more than any other ministry type, requires a 110 percent commitment from the entire family. Church planting is an all-consuming ministry that has its weekly ups and downs. Let no one enter this ministry who is not assessed, called, trained, prepared, and prayed up for the work. Many have tried it and can testify to its rigors. Yet, for the one who is called, it becomes one of the most gratifying things a minister can do.

CROSS-CULTURAL MISSIONARY

Passions: Whether one serves as an evangelist, church planter, administrator, teacher, or pastor, the one thing that all foreign missionaries must possess is what I call a passion for, as well as the accompanying personal resources for, cross-cultural ministry. This is an interest, ability, and even desire to relate to others in another culture. It involves adaptability to new languages and cultures as well as a great sense of mission. I have found that many foreign missionaries recognized this gift before they were ever called to a foreign mission field. Indeed, the presence of the passion itself, in some way, led to their awareness and acceptance of the call. There are other gifts necessary for a foreign missionary, but this gift of cross-cultural aptitude is the most obvious.

Warnings: One might approach foreign missions like a high-school boy dreaming over a Navy recruiting poster: 'Join the Navy and see the world.' Don't do it. Foreign missions, like all types of ministry, requires a deep sense of call; devout commitment to Christ; and because at times the fruit of the ministry is not borne or witnessed for many years, a strong kingdom vision.

INSTITUTIONAL CHAPLAIN

Passions: To be a chaplain is to bring the ministry of the Church to those whose own vocations and situations in life prohibit them from being in a Christian community. A chaplain in a hospital or a prison not only prepares sermons, conducts services, and does visitation like other ministers, but also does so within the context of a given institution. The institution may be a hospital or battlefield or prison, but wherever it is, that institution informs and controls the ministry setting. In short, for chaplaincy, I believe one normally has to have a strong sense of connection to the ministry environment and the people there, as well as for ministry. Thus, as I heard one old chaplain put it, 'I'm not very smart. So when I was deciding what I would do with my life, I knew that a few things would help me decide. Number one, I loved God. Number two, I loved soldiers because I was one. Number three, I could preach. I put those things into my little computer and out came an Army chaplain. And I've been doing that ever since.'

It's hard to imagine anyone putting it any better than that.

Warnings: If you don't love the institution or the people there, this is not the place for you. Go minister in a church or as an evangelist. You will find institutional ministry confining and restrictive unless you have the passion for the institution and the ministry challenges it presents.

A chaplain is not only a pastor, but an evangelist and a missionary. The mission field, if you will, is usually a very distinctive cross-cultural environment (e.g., the military, prison system, healthcare systems).

PARA-CHURCH MINISTER / ADMINISTRATOR

Some ministers are leaders of Christian organizations who work alongside churches to get the gospel out, to disciple new believers, and to facilitate gospel ministry in any number of ways. There are, of course, many specialties needed in para-church ministries. For our concern, I am interested in introducing the work of a minister who labors in administration.

Passion: This person loves the big idea of ministry and recognizes that his contribution is important in seeing it continue. He is chosen by God to lead, to supervise, to conduct and carry out the work of ministry. As with all ordained tasks, in my opinion, this requires a preacher. But, while the administrator may preach and teach in pulpits and classrooms, he is equally at home in casting the vision for the team, the ministry, and leading others to achieve it.

Warnings: Administrators and leaders of Christian organizations do not necessarily get the same preaching and teaching opportunities as their parish counterparts. Furthermore, there is normally no regular administration of the sacraments in this position. There is no liturgical leadership involved with leading a para-church organization. You need to recognize this fact and reconcile it with your own sense of giftedness and calling.

TEACHER / PROFESSOR

Ministers of the gospel have always been at the forefront of instruction and guidance. Teaching, of course, is the very essence of what it is to be an ordained minister. The minister who is a teacher in a secondary school or a professor in a college, university, or seminary not only brings his academic discipline to bear on the students, but also does so with the heart of the preacher.

Passions: Obviously, you must love teaching and students and the thrill of the classroom. Working with other teachers and within the overall goals of the school also plays a crucial part in being happy as a minister-teacher. Moreover, I have found that the one who fits this description also has adapted well to the academic community with its many idiosyncrasies. Because most professors will have done academic work beyond the Master of Divinity degree (i.e., Master of Theology, Doctor of Philosophy, Doctor of Theology), one gets a good opportunity to test the fit while completing graduate study.

Warnings: A teacher in a classroom or a professor in a department is not the same, again, as a pastor in a church. Nor does he only teach. A professor invariably will have to write, research, and work with administration on various projects ranging from recruitment of students to the raising of funds for the school. If you consider that a waste of time when you could be giving the gospel to teenagers in a retreat setting, for example, you obviously need to think about a different color of pulpit.

9

Post Seminary Stress Syndrome
—The crisis of leaving the academy and hitting the field

Hopefully seminary will be a blessed time of preparation. Much of that time will have been spent in the friendships, the collegiality, and the joy of fellowship with other seminarians and their families.

Once you walk the aisle, accept the call or appointment, and settle into your ministry, though, there may, or should I say most probably will, come a time of testing. I call that time of testing the Post Seminary Stress Syndrome. It's not exactly like the post war syndrome where young men struggle with the pressing realities of civilian life even as they reflect upon, have nightmares of, and seek to work out the horrors of the battlefield. But, there are some similarities. There will come some times of reflecting, synthesizing, and sorting out.

I am an Army Reserve chaplain. I was attending a clinic on suicide prevention at The Menninger Clinic as a part of my chaplaincy training. It had been several years since I had left the seminary for my first assignment: church planting. At that time, I had been pastoring the church I had planted and was contemplating another call that had come before me.

The speaker that day, Dr. W. Walter Menninger, was presenting a paper entitled 'Adaptation and Morale: Predictable Responses to Life Change.'[1] Dr. Menninger's presentation that day dealt with the matter of coping with change. Indeed, the research sought to examine the stages of transition in the life of a Peace Corps volunteer from arrival and on through engagement, acceptance, and re-entry (or reassignment to another place of service). I listened intently because, as the physician talked, I had one of those common yet amazing human moments when I felt that he was talking directly to me.

Indeed, the study, which chronicled the morale of individuals, put forth a proposition that this measurement is true of other life changes. I, for one, can validate their study when it comes to transitions into and out of various ministry contexts!

THE STAGES OF THE POST SEMINARY EXPERIENCE

In his study of the experiences and behaviors of Peace Corps volunteers, Dr. Menninger labeled the predictable responses of individuals going through the stages of change as the 'morale curve.' He went on to say that the morale curve is universal.

---

1   W. W. Menninger, 'Adaptation and Morale: Predictable Responses to Life Change,' *Bulletin of the Menninger Clinic* 52, no. 3 (May 1988): 198-210.

As I listened and thought about it, I concluded that what happened to me was exactly what the Menninger Clinic reported had happened to the Peace Corps folks in their study. From talking to other ministers and watching quite a few seminarians, I would say that it happens to all of us in one way or another.

The study was given in order to help chaplains assess the potential for suicide. I trust that no one reading this will even consider that the transition from the seminary to the field leads one to consider suicide. Yet, the feelings that Dr. Menninger describes in his study are quite descriptive of what any of us might go through.

One key to making a smooth transition is adaptability. If we understand the feelings we are experiencing and can recognize that in some way it is even normal to feel these things, we can often adapt and even grow through them. Menninger, in his paper, referred to S.C. Kobasa's 1979 study, in which the author wrote,

> *...those who have a greater sense of control over what occurs in their lives will remain healthier than those who feel powerless in the face of external forces. Part of that control is cognitive control, the ability to interpret, appraise, and incorporate various sorts of stressful events into an ongoing life plan, and, thereby, deactivate their jarring effects.*[2]

With thanksgiving for Dr. Menninger's work, then, I offer his findings and seek to apply them to our situation: the transition from seminarian to minister. I do so with the

---

2   Ibid., page 209. Dr. Menninger is quoting from Suzanne C. Kobasa, 'Stressful Life Events, Personality, and Health: An Inquiry into Hardiness,' *Journal of Personality and Social Psychology* 37, no. 1 (1979), pp. 1-11.

prayer that many will be informed, prepared, and thus spared the jarring effects of that time.

STAGE ONE: THE CRISIS OF ARRIVAL

Menninger wrote that during this stage,

> *...because the individual had entered this situation with deliberation and conscious intent and had survived a selection process, the mood or morale was high. But along with enthusiasm and excitement and sometimes unrealistic euphoria, the volunteers manifested some degree of apprehension and concern about their ability to meet the challenge.*[3]

I had left seminary like a fireball. I had enjoyed a tremendous time of preparation at my own seminary. I had relished the opportunity to immerse myself in study for three years. I had been blessed by mentor relationships with several of my professors. I enjoyed the camaraderie of my fellow seminarians. Having gone to seminary full-time, worked full-time, and interned part-time, I had been living on a very fast-paced schedule for a very long time. My vision of the ministry was big. My expectations of the ministry and for certain immediate results from my ministry were unrealistically high.

As I hit the field—in my case it was to plant a new church—I maintained a strong vision of what I was called to do. However, I suddenly, even abruptly, encountered what Kalervo Oberg called culture shock.[4] This really was shocking to me, because I was from the area where I was

---

3   Ibid., p. 200.

4   Ibid., p. 206.

planting a church! The culture shock had nothing to do with Overland Park, Kansas; it had to do with the abrupt loss of my seminary environs and the loss of peers and mentors to help me interpret my mission and my mission field. I even felt that the loss of my fast-paced schedule—work, school, internship, family all rolled into one—was destabilizing.

I was experiencing:

the anxiety that results from losing all one's familiar cues. These cues include the thousand and one ways in which we orient ourselves to the situations of daily life...[5]

I went forward. I did the work. But I carried a load of loneliness at times that brought despair. In fact, I looked at what was happening to me—a new church being planted, a beautiful home, a new child in our home, a lovely community—and wondered why I should be so down. Sociologist Peter Marris (1975) wrote about this problem:

Since our ability to cope with life depends on making sense of what happens to us, anything which threatens to invalidate our conceptual structures of interpretation is profoundly disruptive ... The impulses of conservatism—to ignore or avoid events which do not match our understanding, to control deviation from expected behavior, to isolate innovation and sustain the segregation of different aspects of life—are all means to defend our ability to make sense of life.[6]

---

5   Ibid., p. 207. See George M. Foster, *Traditional Cultures, and the Impact of Technological Change* (New York: Harper, 1962).

6   Ibid., page 206. See Peter Marris, *Loss and Change* (New York: Pantheon Books, 1974).

I wished I had known then what I know now: There is a powerful emotional impact that comes as one moves through the crisis of arrival. It will not last forever, but it might get worse before it gets better.

STAGE TWO: THE CRISIS OF ENGAGEMENT

How long does all of that take? It depends, of course, but the passage from arrival to engagement may take only four months or so.[7]

In Stage Two, the crisis now intensifies and the uneasiness of Stage One turns rotten. The crisis of engagement reflects the realization of the extent of losses, both real and imagined, in the new situation.[8] The crisis of engagement involves coming to grips with a changed pattern of relationships.[9]

You have lost seminary. You may be in the greatest ministry in the world, but a significant shift has occurred in your life. You had expectations, and things are not exactly going as planned. 'Is this the ministry?' you say to yourself.

You may begin to show symptoms of depression. You spend too much time at Starbucks and not enough time in the study. You have stopped working out. You no longer set the clock at night. You say, 'I'll wake up when I wake up.'

---

7   According to Menninger's Table, 'Comparison of Stages of Adjustment to New Life Situations.' See Table 1 in his paper, page 205.

8   Ibid., page 208.

9   Ibid.

This is a critical time for the minister. All of his training and commitment and sacrifice may be lost in a single decision.

What happens next?

You quit. Or, you go on.

Elizabeth Kubler-Ross, the Roman Catholic nun whose work *On Death and Dying* provides insight into the grieving process, called this stage by another name: *bargaining.* I am not suggesting that my little descriptions of what post-seminary life is like is in any way similar to the social science research of that lady, but I do think her term is helpful. By 'bargaining' I mean to say that there comes a time where the minister 'bargains' within himself about the meaning of it all. Let us be more satisfyingly biblical. There comes a time where one is simply content with one's place. That feeling is too often fleeting. *Christian shepherds can miss the ministry they have been given for the ministry they imagine.*

Remember your Lord's words: I will never leave you nor forsake you. He is with you *where you are today.*

I was winging my way across the Atlantic Ocean for Ph.D. Research in Cardiff, Wales, when, in the midst of my own crisis, I read these words from a book I had providentially brought with me:

> *Whatever stage of a pastor's life you're in, bloom where you're planted. Don't regret it. Don't find fault with it. Don't be obsessed with going to another stage. See what God will do for you where you are. Let Him use your gifts and abilities to His glory, and I'll guarantee you, one day, some time, some place—just as surely as you're reading these words—you'll*

look back on this passage in your ministry and say, Thank you, God. Thank You for giving me the courage. Thank You for giving me the patience. Thank You that I didn't quit.[10]

I commend that to anyone reading these words today. Don't stop. Go on and run the race that is before you. Yes, your losses may be real. But open your eyes as well to the lessons and experiences of your current context, whatever those may be.

STAGE THREE: THE CRISIS OF ACCEPTANCE

Menninger wrote,

The crisis of acceptance reflects the achievement of a new sense of self, with a restructuring of emotional forces and relationships. For most people, this restructuring represents a new equilibrium, with greater freedom...[11]

Eleven to fifteen months have passed. You're through the storm. You are home free. It could be that you saw your crisis for what it was, and I want to discuss that below. It could be that you turned down the other call, deciding not to return to business or industry or the academic life. You determined not to surround yourself with people whom you were sure would tell you what you wanted to hear. Instead, you braced yourself for truth and the wounds of a true friend.[12]

---

10 Loudon, Jr., H.B., Editor, *Refresh, Renew, Revive* (Colorado Springs, CO: Focus on the Family Publishing, 1996) 196.

11 Menninger, *Adaptation*.

12 'Faithful are the wounds of a friend, But the kisses of an enemy are deceitful' (Prov. 27:6).

Now is when your training and your relationships and the nurturing years of seminary life really pay dividends. You might also say that this is the point when your theology takes on legs. You now synthesize reality and theory.

The real beneficiaries of this move are your parishioners, whoever they are. For now, your sermons will take on a fresh delivery. Your illustrations will be more colorful, your applications wiser. Menninger says that this time is marked by activism. You are productive again, maybe for the first time since seminary.

Look close and you'll find that you are also happy again.

STAGE FOUR: THE CRISIS OF RE-ENTRY

This stage only happens if there is a conclusion to your ministry. For many of us there will be. It may be precipitated by any number of events, but at some point you recognize that the Spirit who called you into the ministry is now urging you to follow Him through a new door.

This time, you will note that there is a great difference in the way you are processing the call. In Stage Two, you were ready to run. You were discontent. You were anxious. You were moving toward depression.

Now, if in fact one ministry is ending and another beginning, you are walking with the Lord. You are exploring God's calling with a healthy head and heart.

Just remember. Every change will signal the possible—yea, probable—trigger that will launch you again into another cycle of stages. Remember? This is supposed to be predictable.

But, now you know.

I believe that the result of education is the accumulation of metaphors and constructs and paradigms. We then use these patterns as tools to help us interpret our experiences. The person who has the most metaphors in the quiver is the most educated. The person who knows which metaphor, which construct or paradigm, to draw from the quiver at the appropriate time, is a wise person indeed.

May you go forward in your ministry richly endowed with such wisdom. Be alert to the changes and challenges that you will face at each stage of a transition. Consider these things prayerfully and in conversation with people who know and love you.

CRISIS AS A WORK OF THE SPIRIT

Earlier I wrote of the prized place in which we see things for what they are.

Perhaps what happens to us is not as clinical as it might seem. Perhaps it is not simply a study of empirical data and predictable behavioral science. Perhaps it is the continuing work of the Spirit!

The ministry of Jesus began with a baptism. But not just a baptism. According to the Scriptures, His inauguration into the public ministry for which He was sent to earth was a supernatural event that was accompanied by the Holy Spirit coming down like a dove, a voice from heaven. His calling, His ministry, His mission was affirmed. But, then, the scriptural record takes a sharp turn from the baptism to the wilderness:

'Then Jesus was led up by the Spirit into the wilderness to be tempted by the devil' (Matt. 4:1).

Mark puts it another way:

Immediately the Spirit drove Him into the wilderness (Mark 1:12).

This is an amazing passage to consider. The Third Person of the Trinity drives the Second Person of the Trinity into a wilderness to be tempted by the evil one.

We know that Satan came against the Son of God in those forty days. We may quickly read through the narrative without sensing the aching hunger, imagining the parched mouth, the sun-stroked brow, and the easy way out that was always a possibility before the Creator-in-flesh.

…If You are the Son of God, throw Yourself down… (Matt. 4:6).

But Christ answered each temptation with the Word of God. Every fiery dart was quenched.

We are no better than our Master. If He, oh wonder of wonders, went from the voice of the Father and the anointing of the Spirit in public baptism to the voice of Satan and the abandonment of the Spirit in an isolated wilderness cell, shall we hope to do better?

Could it be that your Post Seminary Stress Syndrome is really a gracious act of the Lord, preparing you, humbling you, refining you, and, yes, even blessing you?

Remember that the story ends with angels coming to minister to the Lord in the wilderness. So too will the

Lord provide for you at every step of your journey of following Him.

I testify to you, dear reader, that I have enjoyed that sweet consolation. I have passed through the wilderness of the early ministry years. But, what I once cursed in my spirit, I now embrace as a gift. For had I never endured the dreaded stages of the Syndrome, those heart-wrenching days of hunger, thirst, and temptation to take the easy way out, I would have never experienced the succor of angels.

10

How to Lose Your Ministry while Excelling in Your Profession
—A tongue-in-cheek call to servanthood in the ministry

The professionalization of the ministry is a constant threat to the offense of the Gospel. It is a threat to the profoundly spiritual nature of our work.—John Piper[1]

I challenge everyone considering the ministry, or for that matter everyone who is engaged in the work of the pastorate, to mark this verse and consider it well:

Therefore, I endure all things for the sake of the elect, that they also may obtain the salvation which is in Christ Jesus with eternal glory (2 Tim. 2:10).

This is a verse that will give us perspective as we enter the ministry, but will also sustain us as we persevere and endure in it.

KEEPING UP APPEARANCES OR PROFESSIONALISM WITHOUT HEART

My wife and I used to really enjoy the BBC comedy hit,

---

1   *Brothers, We are Not Professionals* (Nashville, Tennessee: Broadman & Holman, 2002), 3.

'Keeping Up Appearances.' It was the story of an upper middle income woman named Hyacinth Bucket (which she pronounced with unrestrained pride 'Bouquet') who struggles to maintain the façade of high society in the presence of lesser mortals. At exactly the right moment in each show, when she is trying to impress her neighbors with her good taste, along come her very low society relatives to blow her cover!

The Methodist clergyman and writer Charles Merrill Smith wrote a tongue-in-cheek book for preachers a few decades ago entitled *How to Become a Bishop Without Being Religious*.[2] It was a poignant satire about keeping up appearances while sacrificing your ministry. Smith essentially shows that, like Hyacinth, keeping up appearances in the ministry is a sham.

I want to borrow his approach to express the truth of God's Word with respect to a potentially devastating and most often silent killer in the ministry: professionalism without a heart.

I do not mean to say that we are not to be professional. I do not mean to charge that those of us who seek to improve our ministries through education and associating with others in the ministry are necessarily wrong to do so. For certainly, if we are improving, then it stands to reason that we will serve our people better.

What I mean when I say professionalism without heart is that condition of ministers (and I believe that

2   Charles Merrill Smith, *How to Become a Bishop Without Being Religious* (Garden City, New York: Doubleday and Company, 1965).

154

we are all subject throughout our lives to this insufferable propensity) that prioritizes utility over passion.

To put it another way, professionalism without heart means to do ministry without getting dirty.

Paul must have known that Timothy faced this possibility. In our passage, the apostle encourages the younger minister to be extravagant with his service to the saints at Ephesus. He calls for a hands-in-the-dirt approach to ministry.

We need to hear this today. You and I both know that we can lose our ministries and still excel in our professions as ministers and church leaders.

In keeping with the spirit of Smith's sarcastic title, I want to show you from God's Word how to lose your ministry and actually excel in your profession.

Follow me closely.

YOU CAN LOSE YOUR MINISTRY AND EXCEL IN YOUR PROFESSION IF YOU DO IT THE EASY WAY (2 TIM. 2:3)

In 2 Timothy 2:3 Paul says that we are to '…endure hardship as a good soldier of Christ Jesus.'

Paul uses the metaphor of a soldier in warfare. When Paul writes 'endure hardship,' I know what he means.

I remember that in my officer basic training as an Army Reserve chaplain, we had to crawl under live fire on a beach about one hundred yards long. I remember the horror of the sound of incoming missiles. It was a struggle to crawl beneath fences and around exploding bunkers. I remember saying that if I got to the end of that beach without getting hurt, I would never want to soldier again! Of course, as soon as I got my breath again, we had to head out in a night patrol through a dense forest and endure the tension of possible booby traps and the ever-present hazard of enemies hiding in the brush coming out to attack us. Now, it was all training and not real. But, I can tell you that I slept well when we finally returned that night. Soldiering is hard work!

Each of us who is called to preach the gospel of Christ and to labor in governing the spiritual affairs of the church of Jesus Christ has the responsibility to fight the good fight of faith as soldiers. Seeking to lead a people in God's Word is like crawling across a beach under live fire while the world sends over a few missiles! Disease and sinful attitudes and a plethora of counseling issues fire at you even as you seek to teach the people God's way. It seems that as soon as you get a program going that will result in discipleship, Satan or the world or the flesh throws another grenade at you!

Soldiering is hard work, and so is pastoring. My dearly beloved, in case you haven't figured it out yet, if you aren't careful, it can make you look like a fool! Crawling around on a beach avoiding fire while trying to secure a beachhead is not usually done with a lot of grace and finesse. And I can assure you that trying to bring the gospel to a community while being ambushed by Satan at every move can also make you look less than professional at times! My dear friends, you very well know that you can lose your jobs trying to advance the Word of God in our day, to people who might have come to the place where they enjoy the sins that you are exposing!

Thank God, though, that we have the right weaponry: The Word of God!

Praise be to Christ that our victory is sure in the sovereign hand of Almighty God!

Glory be to the Lord that the Commander in Chief of our Army is the Lord God of Hosts and every enemy shall fall before His mighty plan is finished!

But, just in case you are more concerned about your career than your calling, let me suggest a few steps to help you:

IDENTIFY DIFFICULTIES BEFORE THEY CONFRONT YOU.

By identifying the fact that a given course of action could result in possible danger to your career, you can easily avoid crushing defeat by just avoiding the territory altogether. For instance, if you haven't gathered this by now, by avoiding any teaching on financial stewardship you can avoid a whole host of potential difficulties.

STEER CLEAR OF DIFFICULT PEOPLE.

The second way to avoid a problem in your career is to follow the advice of one church consultant I heard: Choose whom you lose. That is, identify those people who are difficult and get rid of them. Force them to leave, somehow, so you don't have to minister to them. Never mind that their behavior may be concealing deep pain; let another minister who doesn't have a professional image to uphold deal with them!

Avoid Standing for What Could Very Well Cause You to Lose Sleep.

This third way of doing it the easy way is designed to get the most out of life! When you consider that the value of a good night's sleep is worth more than getting involved with sleep-depriving, difficult issues such as figuring out how to minister to the handicapped in your community and how to reach the unchurched in the two-mile area around your church, you will soon be on your way to a more professional image. After all, baggy eyes and a wrinkled brow don't do anything for your photo in the community news section of the local paper!

YOU CAN LOSE YOUR MINISTRY AND EXCEL IN YOUR PROFESSION IF YOU WILL JUST DO IT THE POPULAR WAY (2 Tim. 2:4)

The Apostle tells us that 'No one engaged in warfare entangles himself with the affairs of *this* life, that he may please him who enlisted him as a soldier' (2 Tim. 2:4).

The minister of the gospel, the church leader, every Christian in whatever place, must have a single-mindedness about his or her duty to carry out the Great Commission. Our motivation is to please God. Paul is saying, 'Timothy, there are many lures out there that can rob you of your priorities as a pastor, and one of them is to seek to please others. Do not yield to the temptation. When you pastor, dear boy, you are to do so with an eye on pleasing God.'

Now, I'm going to tell you a story if you promise not to tell anyone else. When I was playing baseball in little league, I had a great coach. I would do anything to please that man. When I was in center field and a pop fly came to me, I would run and catch it, and then I would just look over to 'Mr. Sonny' for his approval. One day, I knew there was a girl from my class sitting in the bleachers. Now, this girl was a beauty. She was clearly out of my league, but I thought that if I could just wow her with my athletic prowess, I could get her attention. Pleasing her (of course, she had no idea who I was and I subsequently proved that she didn't care) was the only thing I could think of when another ball was hit in my direction.

I was going to have to dive for the ball to catch it (but what a wonderful opportunity to impress that gal!). So, I did. I barely caught it, but I nabbed it like a pro! I came up and with great dramatic flair raised the ball in the air to show her and everyone one else that I had miraculously caught it! The problem was that in the midst of my grand performance, the man on third tagged up, and with me taking a bow in the outfield, he trotted on into home plate and scored the winning run. 'Mr. Sonny,' my coach, got real angry. He benched me, and the girl had left the game to get a snow cone and never saw my performance anyway.

Isn't that the way it is in the ministry? We seek to do it the popular way when God tells us to do it His way. Paul says that we are to please our Commander, not the civilian world! In preparing our sermons, are we seeking to please God or show off the fact that we know Greek? When we sign up for our doctoral courses, are we seeking to become educated in order to please God or to impress the next pulpit committee? When we show up at the sickbed of our parishioners, are we there to communicate the love and healing of Christ to hurting people, or to show our church leaders, finally, just how hard we work? When we get an opportunity to preach to our peers, do we do it to wow them or just to be obedient to the One who has called us to preach?

Too often, we have made a decision in the ministry that we hoped would make us look good to a watching world, only to disregard God's plan for our ministries. It's a wonder He doesn't bench us all!

By His grace, may we resolve this day to work as unto the Lord and not unto men.

Of course, we can disregard the apostle's Spirit-inspired words here, and do it the popular way. How is that?

IMPRESS YOUR PEERS

We all want to be admired. Why not use churches as stepping stones to get that perfect pulpit that will make everyone else envious! Then your natural abilities will be obvious to all. Some may even believe that you are God's greatest gift to your denomination and the next superstar!

PATRONIZE YOUR PARISHIONERS

Of course, you must do this one! With just a little reading on Machiavellian technique, all of us can learn how to make our parishioners feel better about themselves, enough to leave us alone so we can spend time doing whatever it is we really want to do!

PLEASE POTENTIAL MEMBERS

We all know that you won't find anyone admitting this in a church growth manual, but, hey, we're all professionals here, right? Avoid the sinner stuff, get around those pesky vows of membership, and just make them feel that as long as they keep their pet sins private, we're not concerned about them.

But, then again, there is that tricky little statement in 2 Timothy 2:4 that no one serving as a soldier gets involved in civilian affairs; he wants to please his commanding officer.

YOU CAN LOSE YOUR MINISTRY AND STILL EXCEL IN YOUR PROFESSION IF YOU WILL ONLY DO IT YOUR WAY! (2 TIM. 2:5)

Second Timothy 2:5 says, 'And also if anyone competes in athletics, he is not crowned unless he competes according to the rules.'

The notes to the old Geneva Bible on this verse provide our interpretation:

> *The ministry is similar to a game in which men strive for the victory, and no man is crowned, unless he strive according to the laws which are prescribed, be they ever so hard and painful.*

All of you Olympic buffs, answer this: What do the Olympic committees do with people who win foot races while on performance enhancing drugs? That happened several years ago in Seoul, South Korea. What happens to a weight lifter on steroids? Of course, their victory is ruled ineligible. They are dismissed from the games under a cloud of shame. They could have been crowned with a garland and a gold medal. Instead they are remembered as phonies and as disgraces to their countries.

The rules of ministry are easy. Carry out your charge, whatever it is, in spirit and in truth with an eye for God's glory. That means different things to different people. For the church planter, it means establishing your church upon God's Word, not upon gimmicks and easy steps to success. For the pastor, it means building ministries that will reach the lost and edify the saints, not just quick fixes to prop you up until you can advance to your next pastorate. For the church leader, it may mean actually getting involved with helping to shepherd the flock rather than just acting as an occasional glorified business consultant.

Naturally, this way of doing things can cost you dearly and even rob you of your professional image. But, if you choose to forego doing it God's way, you will actually lose your ministry. You will miss the crown which He will give to His faithful servants on that Day when He judges the living and the dead. Isn't it much better to labor and toil for the prize and go to sleep at night knowing you are on the right track, no matter how difficult, than to do it your way?

But for those of you intent on doing it your way, here, again, are some pragmatic tips for a sure-fire victory in the profession, without all the hazard of true ministry [tongue, back, firmly in cheek, again:]

Think of Yourself as the First One to Ever Do It
Translation: church history is not for you! What did C.S. Lewis call it? 'Chronological snobbery?' Awe.

Poppycock! This is the twenty-first century and you are in control of your own success or failure. Don't spend any time researching the past or considering the wisdom of previous ministers. Times have changed, and surely you know best.

AVOID THE COUNSEL OF OTHERS.

After all, they are not responsible for building your nest egg. How will you make it up the ladder if you have pious friends warning you against what will obviously place you above them? Forget them! Aren't you doing this for your family's benefit?

RATIONALIZE AWAY EXAMPLES OF HOW GOD'S SERVANTS IN THE BIBLE DID IT

If your conscience bothers you after reading of how Joseph did it God's way rather than his way and yet still came out on top, then just consider that Joseph never got an article on 'Career Management' published in his denominational magazine either!

But, I must call you back to these words: 'And also if anyone competes in athletics, he is not crowned unless he competes according to the rules' (2 Tim. 2:5).

YOU CAN LOSE YOUR MINISTRY WHILE EXCELLING IN YOUR PROFESSION IF YOU DO IT THE LEAST MESSY WAY (THAT IS, WITHOUT GETTING TOO INVOLVED) (2 TIM. 2:6–10)

I come to my final point, and it is concerned most of all with our degree of involvement in the lives of others.

Therefore I endure all things for the sake of the elect, that they also may obtain the salvation which is in Christ Jesus with eternal glory (2 Tim. 2:10).

I must admit that I can imagine Paul saying that he would endure all for the sake of the glory of Jesus Christ! I can expect the great apostle to admit that the cause of the gospel motivates him to endure all things. I can believe that Paul would say that he will undergo persecution for the honor of God... but, it is shocking for me to hear him say that 'I endure everything for the sake of the elect.'

I am startled because I know that people can hurt you in the ministry. I think it is true that people can use you in the ministry. And I am not naturally inclined to give up everything for such people. I am not even compelled to give up much for people who like me, much less for people who use me! I am hard-pressed to suffer for my own relatives, much less for nations and regions and peoples that have nothing even closely related to my life! But that is what Paul is saying. His ministry is driven by sacrificial love for others, that they might obtain eternal life in Jesus Christ.

Now, let me stick my clerical tongue-in-cheek for one final admonition.

Dear friends, this is perhaps the greatest risk to your career—to give your life for evil people. It will ruin you! To risk your professional image on people who could never appreciate your homiletic brilliance or your keen perception of the flow of history or your scholarly grasp of Hebrew syntax is to 'cast your pearls before swine'! Come and let us reason together and let me show you how to keep your professional image secure:

DO MINISTRY WITHOUT GETTING INVOLVED WITH PEOPLE

Most people have not been to seminary and do not understand the real issues in the life of a church. Skip them and you can manage your future much easier and a whole lot quicker.

DO MINISTRY WITHOUT GETTING INVOLVED WITH THEIR PROBLEMS

Can you imagine how far you can go if you don't have to spend your emotional energies on couples facing divorce or singles facing loneliness issues or people struggling to understand what you mean when you preach?

DOCTORS OR HEALERS?

The time has come to switch back to reality. This is, quite obviously, just the opposite of what Paul is saying when he says he endures all for the sake of the elect. But, does his statement really characterize your understanding of your ministry?

You and I know that there is a temptation to define success in a way that is just the opposite of what God requires for our ministry, and you and I know that one can do it and still get nominated for Clergyman of the Year!

But such success comes at a high price. It is time for my little exercise to come to an end. Let me get very serious in closing.

I saw a movie the other day that centered on the life of a medical school community. It involved a young man who was struggling with his call to become a physician.

At the end of the movie, there was a quote which really grabbed me.

I made doctors, but people need healers.

It grabbed my heart because it was spoken by a medical school faculty member who, in dealing with her own inoperable and terminal disease, found that the very men she had trained were quite professional but without the slightest evidence of compassion for her as a suffering patient. She looked at one of those young men who was struggling with his call to be a doctor. It was that woman, that faculty member, who told a young medical student, 'I made doctors, but people need healers.' When she spoke those poignant words, she seemed to be telling him, 'Don't be just another professional physician. They lack the heart and soul that is truly needed by a patient who is gripped by fear of the unknown and who is placing her life in his hands! Be a healer! Have a heart for your patients! Show us that we are not just another manila folder in your clinical file cabinet!'

I made doctors, but people need healers.

I looked at my life and my ministry. I was growing in my profession while all the while possibly distancing myself from the real-life pains of my people. I was diagnosing their spiritual conditions without weeping for them. I was getting professional without heart.

Some of us are clergymen, but people need healers.

Others of us are professional board members of the church, but people need care givers.

How different we often are from the apostle Paul, who said, '… I endure all things for the sake of the elect, that they also may obtain the salvation which is in Christ Jesus….' What beatings and insults and deprivation of every human comfort was Paul's for the sake of other people! Paul was imitating Christ, who said He came to serve and to give His life as a ransom for many! And he tells us in Philippians that we must imitate Jesus Christ. Our Lord left His royal robes of heaven to come and take on the poverty-stricken conditions of a carpenter in an occupied country. He offered His body and His blood as a sacrifice of unimaginable love for a people who were sinners and who even hated Him to death!

You can be a raging success and still lose your passion for souls, which is your ministry.

Of course, you will never be happy. Of course, you will one day die and have to face the truth that it was not worth it. Of course, you will regret not having given your all to the ministry to which Almighty God had called you. For if God has called you to be an ambassador for His kingdom and to plead with the hearts and minds of men to embrace Jesus Christ, you will never be happy until your life is in every way poured out as an offering for the sake of God's elect.

Dearest fellow laborers in Christ, please go ahead and commit yourself to improving your ministry. Become a sharper instrument in the hands of Him who called you. But do it while getting your hands dirty in the rich soil of human lives which are in desperate need of someone like you who is willing to love them and help them to obtain the salvation that is in Christ Jesus with eternal glory.

Seek God's forgiveness if you have failed. Receive your renewal in Him and recover your passion for the ministry to which God has called you. Do it right now before you go any further in this day.

In the name of the Father and of the Son and of the Holy Spirit. Amen.

11

The Life Cycle of a Pastor
—According to the ministry of
St Paul

*It is said that in some countries trees will grow, but will
bear no fruit, because there is no winter there. The Lord bless
all seasons to his people, and help them rightly to behave
themselves, under all the times that go over them—John
Bunyan.*[1]

The ministry of the Apostle Paul, as recorded in Scripture,
affords one example of a pastoral life cycle. It is suggestive,
and prescriptive, of how we who are called as pastors may
be stewards of our ministries.

One caveat: this is suggestive; certainly holds expository
truths, but recognizing that God in His sovereignty could
cause our ministerial career to look more like St. Stephen's.
We do not move through each of these stages with
a guarantee, because death waits for no man. Also, the
tide of affairs in the life of a minister may overwhelm

---

1   Elliot Ritzema and Elizabeth Vince, eds., *300 Quotations for
Preachers from the Puritans*, Pastorum Series (Bellingham,
Washington: Lexham Press, 2013).

the movement from one stage in the cycle to another. So we offer this with prayer and dependence upon the God who calls and the God who sustains. It is, we say again, suggestive.

The five-part movement (Figure 1) is intended to reflect the movements observed in St. Paul's ministry. These movements are discussed below.

STAGES OF THE PASTOR'S LIFE CYCLE

1. CONVERSION (ACTS 9:1-19)
The future pastor is spiritually re-born as he trusts in Jesus Christ. 'He is the Son of God' (Acts 9:20). There can be no divine call without a sacred encounter with the living Christ. The Season gives way into the next stage quite intentionally.

2. CALLING AND PREPARING (GAL. 1:17)
In the spiritually youthful season of faith, the believer begins a veritable wrestling with God over the internal and the external call. The divine call to ordained ministry may be incremental, or Pauline-like (a sudden awakening to the reality of this call) or it may manifest itself in a variety of other expressions. Yet, the call, once affirmed, internally and externally, moves to preparation. As St. Paul experienced his own time of preparation, you, too, will come to a sacred time of waiting on the Lord as you learn. That is the place of 'seminary,' or a more apprentice-based phase. Yet, Calling and Preparing go together and one must always look back to say of his own life, 'I went away into Arabia…Then after three years I went up to

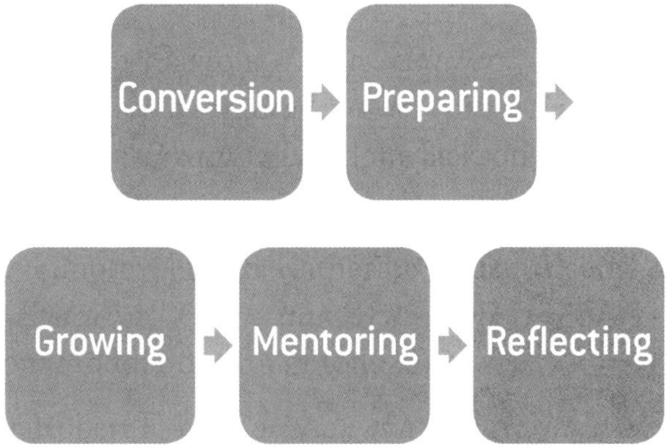

Figure 1. The life cycle of a pastor according to the ministry of St. Paul.

Jerusalem...' (Gal. 1:17-18). Thus, there is an undeniable necessity to humbly yield yourself to a prolonged season of vocational guidance in character and competency.

This season moves into the next by completion of necessary education. This is a decision that is, also, realized in the community of elders in the ministry. For 'no man takes this honor unto himself' (Heb. 5:4).[2]

3. GROWING (ACTS 13:13)

Then comes the obligation to faithfully move to the fields of ministry. Whether as a pastor, missionary, or through some other expression of ministry, the newly ordained Christian shepherd moves from the cocoon of preparation under more senior ministers to a time of productivity. This time is equal to the Sundays after Pentecost in the Church Year. This 'green season' is one of of growth and expansion.

Caution should be taken at this point: the first years after seminary (or however that season of preparation was wrought in your life) should be carefully monitored. Why? There are pitfalls aplenty. There are opportunities abounding. Yet, you are young in the ministry. No doubt, your zeal competes with your practical wisdom for good decisions. What must be done? Let me put it this way: as a medical doctor moves from medical school to 'residency,' from learning the anatomy of the subject to the experiential dynamics of the subject, so, too, the minister of the Gospel should spend time in a residency of sorts for Christian

---

2   The *D. James Kennedy Institute for Reformed Leadership* is one such place to discover an intentional program for 'pastors-in-residence.' For more information see http://djkleader.org/.

shepherds. This, prayerful, long season transitions to the next by a providential event. The 'green' phase of ministry transitioned in the life of St. Paul through persecution, imprisonment, and awaiting execution. 2 Timothy is a remarkably moving epistle in which Paul recognizes the transition. 'Change is psychologically painful,' wrote Margo A. Denke, M.D. of the University of Texas.[3] The Christian shepherd has many resources to help navigate the emotionally treacherous shoals of this new stage of ministry. Yet, change is at the heart of the transition. Whether by health, aging, or merely stepping back from a demanding schedule, the issue of a personal calling of God is forever entangled, most understandably, with the minister's identity. For so long the week-to-week rhythms of sermon and worship preparation, as well as counseling, pastoral visitation, and, perhaps, guiding a Christian community, have been a veritable source of sanctification. Yet, the change does not have to mean a conclusion to ministry, but merely, and happily, a new opportunity.

4. MENTORING *(2 TIM. 2:1-2)*

Paul was a mentor to Timothy: 'You then, my child, be strengthened by the grace that is in Christ Jesus' (2 Tim. 2:1, ESV) Yet, this mentoring is not merely an act of conveying information or seasoned wisdom to a younger pastoral practitioner. The context for Paul's mentoring

---

3   Margo A. Denke, 'Book Review—Aging Well: Surprising Guideposts to a Happier Life' *New England Journal of Medicine,* 347, no. 2 (2002): p. 150.

comes out of a robust transition that has happened in his life.

I like to refer to this new stage of ministry using the term that one psychiatrist coined for the missing element in Erikson's *Stages of Human Development:*[4] 'the Keeper of Meaning.'[5] This is a time of 'conservation and preservation' of the collective wisdom of Christian shepherding and, indeed, the caretaking and guardianship of the traditions and meaning of pastoral life in the Christian Church.[6] 'The Keeper of Meaning'—guarding the deposit, caretaking through wise instruction—is, I believe, a very apt and faithful phrase that might also be described by what we see in 2 Timothy: *mentoring*.

This season transitions into the next by providential events (in the case of St. Paul, through his continued imprisonment).

5. REFLECTING *(2 TIM. 4:7-8, 17-18)*

Oh, what sweet words of comfort for the one entering this new stage of ministry: 'But the Lord stood by me and strengthened me, so that through me the message might be fully proclaimed…' (2 Tim. 4:17, ESV): this becomes the final (earthly) stage in the development or lifecycle of the Christian shepherd. Yet, this season is by no means

---

4   Erik H. Erikson, *Identity and the Life Cycle* (New York: W.W. Norton, 1980).

5   Dr. George Vaillant (1934-) is an American psychiatrist who contributed this stage as what he has observed as a missing stage in Erikson's Stages of Development.

6   'Conservation' and 'preservation' being terms borrowed from Dr. Vaillant's book.

less meaningful than the others. The difference between the 'green' season of ministerial effectiveness and the possible strength of the season of reflecting is only time. 'Only time.' Two words describe a remarkable transition. Yet, is there not power in this stage, if the pastor has built a life of service to God and Man? It is in this stage that his reflections may become the wisdom that guides the next generation of shepherds. We don't do well with aging in the West. We idolize youth at our own expense. For the white-headed Christian shepherd, perhaps, bent over in pain, certainly weakened by a fallen world taking its toll on his 'earthly tent,' may remain a cheerful spirit in the face of death. It is here that a lifetime of ministry becomes the living lesson of faith in Christ before the cavernous darkness of death. And, as John Donne, the poet-preacher of St. Paul's, confronted that period, he deposited remarkable wisdom to those who followed him in the form of his *Sonnet X:*[7]

> *Death be not proud, though some have called thee*
> *Mighty and dreadful, for, thou art not so,*
> *For, those, whom thou think'st, thou dost overthrow,*
> *Die not, poore death, nor yet canst thou kill me.*
> *From rest and sleepe, which but thy pictures bee,*
> *Much pleasure, then from thee, much more must flow,*
> *And soonest our best men with thee doe goe,*
> *Rest of their bones, and souls deliverie.*
> *Thou art slave to Fate, Chance, kings, and desperate men,*

---

7   See, e.g., John Donne, *Devotions upon Emergent Occasions*, ed. Anthony Raspa (New York: Oxford University Press, 1987), xii–xiv.

And dost with poyson, warre, and sicknesse dwell,
And poppie, or charmes can make us sleepe as well,
And better than thy stroake; why swell'st thou then;
One short sleepe past, wee wake eternally,
And death shall be no more, Death, thou shalt die.

Thus, this remarkable season, this winter season, transitions, as Christ may tarry in His return, through death.

VARIABLES AFFECTING THE LIFE CYCLE

This is a very good time for you to put the book down. It is a good time to pray and a perfect time to listen.

Where are you? What *stage* are you in? Are you transitioning from one stage to another? What are the 'controlling' needs in your transition (i.e., how could turning the levers of education be helpful in your stage?)?

What are the challenges inherent with each stage? Is there a more singular sinful condition that is exposed in each respective stage? If so what is that condition? What is the threat level to the hopefulness of a given stage?

Consider each stage from the following 'controls'. Controls (i.e., variables) are 'levers on the dashboard' that can help you successfully navigate the stage. Thus, each of the controls is a dominant area of impact—positively or negatively—in the movement.

Family Life

Ministry demands may likely be more intense in 'Growing' than in other stages.

Life stage (i.e., geriatric health issues) in 'Reflecting' likely creates special family needs during the 'Reflecting' stage.

DEVOTIONAL LIFE

Mentoring stage may be enhanced for greater ministry effectiveness with less text and more meditation on singular Scriptural portions, for example reading one Psalm over an entire week (or month) and using *lectio divina* (or your own tradition's application of that third-century Christian practice)—a slow and thoughtful reading of the Scripture that prayerfully seeks Christ as the interpretive principle of the text—to pray through the Psalm.

RELATIONSHIPS

The 'Reflecting' stage may be enhanced through intentional friendship with a pastor in the 'Growing' stage ('Tuesdays with Morrie') who might choose to journal the reflections.

PHYSICAL LIFE

Keeping fit during the 'growing' season may be used by the Lord to extend that season for greater effectiveness and longer service.

FALLEN CONDITION REALITIES

There is an observable tendency of new Christians in the 'Conversion' stage to be over-zealous and short with others who don't share their own experience of God. As you disciple a believer at this stage, introduce the reading of several spiritual biographies and assign a more mature friend to meet with the convert and reflect on the similarities and differences in the several conversion stories.

EDUCATION OR TRAINING

One might be supported during the 'Growing' stage by a sabbatical, or a return to an educational program, a scholarly degree, or a professional degree like a Doctor of Ministry degree.[8]

Each stage is challenged. Each staged is necessary for the graduation to the next. The final graduation, of course, will be by the Lord to His presence forevermore.

---

8   I advocate framing such times as vocational renewal. If the 'green season' of pastoral productivity is long, then it is wise to find shade under a tree, a willing soul in a more advanced stage, and sit for a while, before returning to the pastoral work. I have observed that when a degree or a sabbatical is approached with such intentionality and with respect for the worth of the time, it brings long-lasting benefits to the pastor, the pastoral family, and the parish.

12

Beginning Your Ministry

Behold! on what sure foundations his happiness is built whose soul is possessed with divine love, whose will is transformed into the will of God, and whose greatest desire is that his Maker should be pleased. O the peace, the rest, the satisfaction that attends such a temper of mind!—Henry Scougal[1]

I don't want this book to be a collection of add-ons to fill up pages. I do hope that we can add some specific messages and writings that might bring the reader some further thought on the matter of vocation. Here is a message from an installation that is a simple one. Perhaps it could be of help as you transition into seminary and out of seminary and into the work of the Church. The message now begins...

The first things that are said at the beginning of a new relationship are the most important. We know that in

---

1   Elliot Ritzema and Elizabeth Vince, eds., *300 Quotations for Preachers from the Puritans*, Pastorum Series (Bellingham, Washington: Lexham Press, 2013).

courtship, in relationships with friends, and even in job interviews and sales appointments. The time of charging a new pastor and the congregation is no different.

The Bible teaches us in 1 John 4:7-12 that 'God is love.' That simple, profound teaching should change everything about your ministry, your church, and your future.

This is the inerrant and infallible word of the living God:

> *Beloved, let us love one another, for love is from God, and whoever loves has been born of God and knows God. Anyone who does not love does not know God, because God is love. In this the love of God was made manifest among us, that God sent his only Son into the world, so that we might live through him. In this is love, not that we have loved God but that he loved us and sent his Son to be the propitiation for our sins. Beloved, if God so loved us, we also ought to love one another. No one has ever seen God; if we love one another, God abides in us and his love is perfected in us (1 John 4.7-12, ESV).*

I once read that Peggy Noonan, former speechwriter for President Ronald Reagan, and now a columnist with the *Wall Street Journal*, declared that the deepest, most profound things in life are said the simplest. For instance, what could be more profound, deep and enduring than the simple words, 'I love you.' Yet as simple and as profound as those words are, even more profound and yet at the same time as simple—childlike, if you will—are the words that John Guest called the most transformative words in the world: 'God loves you.'[2]

2   John Guest, *Knowing You Are Loved: What It Means to Know with Certainty That God Loves You* (Ann Arbor, Michigan: Vine Books, 1987), 5ff.

As you begin your ministry together I want to charge both pastor and congregation to focus on the love of God. And when I say focus on the love of God I want to concentrate on three truths for my charge to you from this text.

LEAD WITH LOVE

We recognize in this text that the word 'love' is repeated several times in this passage. In the original text, this word comes from the root word 'agape,' referring to the covenantal love of God. This is a love like no other, as Martin Luther reminded us in his famous Heidelberg disputation.

The love of human beings is a reactive love. It reacts to impressions of beauty, or kindness, or sympathy, or some other impulse. This is entirely different from divine love. The love of God, which St. John speaks of in this passage, is a creative power independent of people's qualities. God loves out of His own being. All children know the passage contained in this text, 'God is love.' And so He is. And thus He loves us, not based on what we can give to Him, or what beauty He sees in us, or even what potential He may see in us, but He loves us out of Himself. He is love. And that love overflows unto His own creation. Out of that love you and I have been elected unto eternal life.

So, what does a theology of the love of God have to do with pastoring? Or with being the people of God in the world? Or relating to each other as pastor, pastoral family and congregation? Quite simply, everything. For if we focus on God's love, indeed, pastor, if you lead with love, that is, leading with God's love, not with what you find desirable in your people, not with what you find as advantageous for your ministry, but out of the sacred encounter you have had personally with God's love, then the love of God will be perfected in you. In this case, then, your vocation will become your sanctification. In this session, diaconate, women of the church, children of the church, and all the people of the church, as you all walk together in this love, you'll become a congregation that is, literally, out of this world.

How does this work out practically? For this minister of the Gospel, it means that his pastorate, following the love of God, will seek to minister out of nothing else but the love of God. That means when a cranky congregant, or a peeved parishioner sends e-mails to say that they didn't appreciate your closing illustration that you felt was rather brilliant, rather than being deeply offended and hurt you take that to the Lord and you ask how the love of God can be shed abroad in the heart of this one. Maybe you even asked, out of God's love, how can my closing illustrations better show the text? Maybe it wasn't the best close! The bottom line for those of us who preach and pastor is that we must continually examine our motivations for ministry. There have been times when I have asked myself that question and not liked the answer. In such times there must be a recalibration to seek to reflect the love of God in my ministry.

And for the congregation? Leading out of love means bringing the pastor and his family before the God of love each and every day. The love of God was shed abroad, according to this passage, in its most glorious way, through the giving of God's own Son to the world, so that we might live through Him. Therefore, there should not only be the giving of pastor to congregation, there should be the giving of the congregation to the pastor—and I'm not talking about used tea bags or even Christmas bonuses. I'm talking about love. It remains for you to work out the love of God among yourselves. It will be your creative challenge to discover ways of showing love to each other. But each of you must lead not the way the world leads, but lead with love, God's love.

This leads me to my second charge from this passage.

LEAVE IN LOVE

There is an evangelistic component in this passage that causes us to leave, like Christ, and go to the world with the love of God.

This passage says in verse 12 that 'no one has ever seen God; if we love one another, God abides in us and his love is perfected in us.' It seems that the Apostle John is concerned about the role of the congregation in the community. John's theology of love is expressed here in order for the people to understand that as God's love is lived out among them—the redeeming love, the agape love that sent the Lord Jesus Christ to live the life we could never live, die the death which should've been ours, and to liberate captives to sin and death, giving us abundant life and eternal life—so others may know this love. A theology of love at work in a congregation is the beginning of the fulfillment of the Great Commission.

Pastor, as you pastor out of this divine love, not out of a human love, by which I mean a love that is a reactive love (i.e. 'if you don't give me any trouble and let me have a really nice, comfortable pastorate, then I may love you back'), you will know joy inexpressible. If your pastorate is known by love, even more so than by your preaching, or your administering, or your teaching, then hurting, broken people will be attracted. For divine love is not native to this old world. The people only understand human, reactive love, to borrow from Luther once again. When they see or hear about a divine love at work, even though they don't even know what to call that love, they are attracted to it. Indeed, the Holy Spirit draws His elect to the Father as the love of Jesus is manifested through your ministry.

People of God, because of the imperatives in this passage to focus on the love of God and to lead out of that love, you will, naturally, or should I say supernaturally, reach out to your community in that same love. This love bubbled over is the reality of God's love in our lives and it in turn, bubbles over into others. This is the way of divine love.

An old Burt Bacharach classic was, 'what the world needs now is love, sweet love.'[3] And that is true. But it is not the love that is a reactive love, but the impulse of divine love displayed in the Lord Jesus Christ, lived out in His people, and shared with others, in word and in deed.

I will never forget the Rev. Dr. James Baird, former senior minister of First Presbyterian Church, Jackson,

---

3   Burt Bacharach et al., writers, *What the World Needs Now Is—Burt*, Warner Jazz, 2006, CD.

Mississippi, coming to our seminary in my first year there. He spoke to the class and his last words in his pastoral ministry class were, 'if you preach to the broken hearts, you will never lack for a congregation.' I would paraphrase Dr. Baird tonight and say to you, 'if you will preach the love of God to this loveless world, you will never lack a vision or a mission for your Ministry together.'

So pastor and People of God: lead with love, and reach out in love. But to do so will require one last thing, and this is the most important aspect about this passage.

LEARN OF LOVE

Your time together will be a great experiment, if you will. It will require learning how to live together, just as the Saints were doing in the epistle we read, forgiving each other, lifting each other up, and always leaving an empty space for others to join you, as you love one another. The Bible tells us that if you do that, God will abide with you, and His love will be perfected among you. And I say these things so that in your greatest challenges, as well as in your most glorious successes, together as pastor and people, you will always return to these first words, the simple words, these profound words, 'God is love.' And that changes everything.

In the Name of the Father, and of the Son and of the Holy Spirit. Amen.

13

The Double Blessing

I wonder if there is something that is missing in your life as a believer in Christ? As a minister of His Gospel? I wonder if that one missing thing might be the anointing of God?

> *Sow to yourselves in righteousness, reap in mercy; break up your fallow ground: for it is time to seek the LORD, till He come and rain righteousness upon you.(Hosea 10:12)*

> *When they had crossed, Elijah said to Elisha, 'Ask what I shall do for you, before I am taken from you.' And Elisha said, 'Please let there be a double portion of your spirit on me.' (2 Kings 2:9)*

I write to ministers of the Gospel. Yet even if you are not ordained, this theological reflection is for you. There are principles here for every believer whatever one's vocation may be. So I invite you to keep reading.

We lay much due importance on the diligence of our biblical studies, homiletic and pastoral practice. That is good and right. But ask yourself if you are seeking God in prayer for His holy anointing of your ministry. Elisha sought a double portion of Elijah's ministry. God told us to seek Him and we will find Him. The Lord invites us to come to Him for wisdom. He invites us to walk in His Spirit. We need His anointing. We need His blessed hand upon our lives in the way that He blessed the prophets and the apostles and the martyrs.

We study Calvin. But do we pray for the anointing that came upon that man of God? We marvel at Luther's courage, but do we pray for it in our lives? We love to soak up the godly words of the English Puritans, but do we long for their holiness and actually plead with God in earnest prayer that He might bestow such God-besotted language on our tongues? We read Edwards for his brilliance, his pastoral wisdom in discerning between spiritual fruit and diabolical barnacles on a true work of God, but are we regularly pleading with Christ for that wisdom in our lives? We read of how Robert Murray M'Cheyne cultivated such holiness in his life that people were said to come under conviction of the Holy Spirit when they passed him on the street.

Do you seek the Spirit of holiness to fall on you, dear pastor? Seminary student, when you read the bold, *bibline* expository preaching of Charles Spurgeon, do you just read to marvel, or do you read and crave the holy blessing that was on that man? Not for your glory, but for God's glory and for the salvation of lost souls? We read Murray's biography of 'the Doctor' but would we fast before the living God to give us such an anointing as He gave Martyn Lloyd-Jones? We read Dallimore's *Whitefield* and put it down in awe. But why not fall to our knees and plead for that anointing?

So much of our work today seems to me to be of the flesh. We must combine godliness with learning or we will miss the better part. Years ago, when I was preparing for ordination, I happened to also be on a trip to the University of Wales to begin my studies there. I flew into London, went to the Foreign Missions Club, and fell asleep having flown all night and studied along the way. I was awakened to learn that I had a train to catch at Victoria Station that would take me, by night, to Wales.

Having recently graduated from seminary, preparing for both ordination exams and for my first class at the University of Wales doctoral program, I felt compelled by God through prayer to go to the tomb of Charles Haddon Spurgeon. I have an English friend who tells me that he believes that idolatrous American clergymen make pilgrimages over to the UK in order to worship the bones of Spurgeon and other British heroes of the faith! I told him that I was not going to the tomb of Spurgeon, at Norwood Cemetery, to worship the Preacher's bones, but his God. Was God any closer there? No. But 'place' means something in a way that a name means something.

There in front of me lay the entombed remains of the Prince of Preachers and his godly helpmate Susannah. That man of God, anointed for ministry in a most unusual way by the Lord, shall come forth from his tomb as surely as Jesus came forth from His. Spurgeon shall sail into the heavens to be with Christ forever more in a new heaven and a new earth. I thought about his past, the thousands that he baptized, and of the volumes of his printed sermons that we have. I thought about his future as I sat there.

As the darkness and heavy fog of the west side of the Thames began to descend I realized I had a train to catch. The mist turned into rain. I knelt down at that place where he lay. I remembered the promises of God and the blessings that He had bestowed. I asked God right then and there to give me but a thread from the mantle of that man, for I could not wear any more than a thread.

The call. The call amidst the company of other faithful ones who lived out that call. I think this is the double blessing.

14

On Mentors in Ministry

*With correct and established views of propriety in the service,
and a right judgment of its value to the people of God, a well
trained and devout ministry will serve the house of God the
better for the greater freedom.* [1]

You should think carefully about where you are going
to seminary, or Bible College, or the church where you
will do your pastoral internship. The pastor-scholar will
become a mentor. Our understanding of mentor, we
are often told, comes from the character of Mentor in
Homer's *Odyssey*. While the word itself finds it etymon
in the classic Greek epic (and from that rather decrepit
character in it), we know that the relationship it describes

---

1 'Review of *The Directory for the Worship of God* in the Presbyterian
Church in the United States of America, as Amended and
Ratified by the General Assembly, in May, 1841 and *The Book
of Common Prayer, and Administration of the Sacraments, and
Other Rites and Ceremonies of the Church*, according to the
Use of the Protestant Episcopal Church in the United States of
America,' The Biblical Repertory and Princeton Review 19, no.
1–4 (1847): p. 81.

is most certainly grounded in a gracious divine revelation. As Moses was to Joshua and Elijah was to Elisha so we, too, are to another—or should be. We must, therefore, pray, and, then follow the Lord to find that faithful guide who will guide us, through a wise ministry of presence.[2] This dynamic leads one to a place of study for ministry. The result of that relationship then propels one into ministry for the rest of one's natural life.

For purposes of illustrating this most salient feature of preparing for ministry I offer this tribute to one of my mentors who went to be with the Lord.

In these days after Dr. Robert L. Reymond has gone to be with the Lord, I give glory to God in thanksgiving for the life of His Servant. Dr. Reymond preached Christ Jesus as the only Savior and Lord. He faithfully declared the Bible to be a 'Word from another world.' He regularly evangelized 'publicly and from house to house.' Dr. Reymond should be recalled as a great preacher of the Word, a compassionate pastor, an unfailing evangelist, and a constant friend. Dr. Reymond was a beloved husband, father, grandfather, and his family reflects the covenant promises of God. Bob Jr. and Sheri are close friends who were core members of the church we prayed for in Dr. Reymond's living room back in 1990 and his son serves as a ruling elder there now. Dr. Reymond sat under the preaching of Reverend James Baxter, another of his former students (Jim graduated from Covenant Seminary)

---

2   See, e.g., Robert Aubrey and Paul M. Cohen, *Working Wisdom: Timeless Skills and Vanguard Strategies for Learning Organizations* (San Francisco: Jossey-Bass Publishers, 1995).

who will preach his funeral in our home church in Olathe, Kansas; this speaks to the breadth and expansiveness of the great theologian's influence.

Bob and Shirley were well known for their bounding hospitality. My wife and daughter stayed with the Reymonds for three weeks when we moved to seminary. My son spent the first week of his life with us in an extra bedroom in the Reymond home. After almost two decades of faithful teaching at Covenant Theological Seminary, Dr. Reymond had accepted Dr. D. James Kennedy's challenge to help found Knox Theological Seminary in Fort Lauderdale. Dr. Reymond, with Drs. George Knight, Joseph Hall, and Laird Harris, became a popular teacher and a frequent preacher in the pulpits of Coral Ridge and other congregations in South Florida.

We went through Hurricane Andrew together and I heard Shirley say, 'Wake up, Bob, you just slept through the worst natural disaster in American history.' To which Dr. Reymond responded, 'Shirley, a good conscience allows for good sleep anytime, anywhere.' When I was ordained he was there. When I planted our first and second churches, he was there at the dedication services. He taught me, counseled me, and tutored me in pastoral ministry. Indeed, while he is being recalled as one of the greatest systematic theologians of our time, for those like myself, who sat under his teaching, he was preeminently a pastoral theologian. All theology, for Dr. Reymond, ultimately, was pastoral and applied.

Truly Dr. Reymond is remembered as a man who be-lieved and taught the Westminster Confessional standards as the very Gospel of Jesus Christ. That Gospel transformed his life and thousands of other lives of ministers who preach today.

As the mantle of Dr. Kennedy falls upon me to preach the Truth that Transforms, I am remembering that Dr. Reymond has now joined Dr. Kennedy in the Church Triumphant. The Truth has now transformed *and translated.*

Dr. Reymond had a 'life verse' and encouraged his students to also consider applying a verse to one's life. When he recited his, tears came to his eyes. Now, tears are coming to mine.

I am crucified with Christ: nevertheless I live; yet not I, but Christ liveth in me: and the life which I now live in the flesh I live by the faith of the Son of God, who loved me, and gave himself for me (Gal. 2:20, KJV).

15

Renewing Your Call to Ministry[1]

We all love to beat up on Peter. He is unbridled, brag-gadocious, embarrassingly bold, and, at times, violent. But he is also a man who was greatly used of God, to preach at Pentecost, to lead the Church at Jerusalem, to minister to the Church at Rome, to minister to suffering saints in Asia Minor. In other words he is like us. He leans on self to minister at times and then has to turn again, or even be turned by Paul, to lean on grace. He is just a preacher. The account of Peter's renewal and re-commissioning by Jesus is found in John 21:1-22.

'What is God doing in my life, in my ministry? I just don't know.'

My friend, a chaplain who has been deployed twice in three years, a husband, father, godly man, never fails to

---

1 The following chapter was first written as a sermon given to 'Military Chaplains and Spouses on Spiritual Retreat at The Cove' (Billy Graham Evangelical Association, Asheville, North Carolina) in December, 2009.

listen to the soldier who drops in to talk about a family matter, or a job matter, or to just chat about a ball game. He is the kind of chaplain who sees ministry just beneath the surface of the old master sergeant who wants to talk about the Monday night football game or to laugh with the first lieutenant as he recounts his nervousness on his first Thanksgiving with his fiancé's family. He is a good chaplain. But he is wondering about God's call on his life.

I think that if we admit it, we can identify at some level with my friend. We all, at one time or another, have a Gethsemane moment, when the pressures and the realities of the ministry to which we are called collide with the people we know ourselves to be. Sometimes it happens when friends are killed and we are not. Sometimes it happens when we do our best and get bad OERs (Officer Evaluation Report). Sometimes it is when we are at our best and get a bad MRI.

'What is God doing in my life, in my ministry?' And we say with my friend, 'I just don't know.'

I would say that 'poor-in-spirit' is not a bad place to be, but rather a good place to be. It is a place where God can use us in even greater ways. But there are things, Gospel things, sacred-encounter things, that must happen in order to hear God's answer to our dark night-of-the soul plea for understanding. And where do we turn?

John is a Gospel storyteller. He is the one we always point to when we are witnessing to someone who needs the Lord, right? 'Just read a little bit of John every night before bed.' We know that God's Word doesn't return void. And we know that John will always deliver. For John's purpose statement in his Gospel is clear:

> *But these are written so that you may believe that Jesus is the Christ, the Son of God, and that by believing you may have life in His name. (John 20:31)*

But John ends his Gospel with a story of resolution. The resolution of the call of Peter. And it is here where all ministers of Christ, military chaplains or parish pastors, vicars in country churches and senior pastors of mega-churches, and presidents of seminaries, must fall into the arms of Jesus again. In John 21 the Lord provides a safe haven for pastors to lay down their stoles and listen to the quiet, sweet voice of Jesus guiding us to renew our commitment to our call from Him.

I almost called this chapter *Renewing Your Passion for Your Ministry*. But then the Lord showed me in this passage that this is not really about our passion; it is about His passion for His ministry through us. In fact, Peter's problem and often ours, is our passion for our ministry, rather than our love of the One who so passionately desires to minister His Gospel to the world. So I see in John 21:1-21 how God meets us at the point of our need as ministers to renew our commitment to His call on our lives.

There are four words that I want to use to describe the sacred movements in this passage that bring about that renewal of calling.

REFLECTION

We all know this passage. Peter has blasphemed the Savior, denied Him, run away from Him. And so we find Peter here telling Thomas, Nathanael and John and another disciple, 'I am going fishing' (John 21:3). It is here that I have sometimes said, 'Now, this man who was so foolishly bold at one time, has given up and is just going back to what he knew before. He is giving up on the ministry.' I have been in ministry long enough to know that this is not the best way to handle this. To hear this man saying, 'I am going fishing' is to hear the echo of his words in my own heart, when a session meeting has gone bad, or my latest, greatest ministry program went sour, or I have ministered so much in my own strength instead of Christ's strength, that I am just depleted. 'I am going gardening.' 'I am going hunting.' 'I just want to get away.'

Remember that this Peter who had denied Jesus, after bragging that the rest of the disciples might do that, but he never would, is the same Peter who ran with John to see the empty tomb. He saw the face cloth that had been on Jesus' head. He saw the winding sheets all 'folded up in a place by itself' (John 20:7). Peter must have been with the disciples when the resurrected Christ came through locked doors on that first day of the week when He said, 'Peace be with you' (John 20:19). Peter must have heard Jesus say, 'As the Father has sent Me, even so I am sending you' (John 20:21). And those words must have burned into the core of Peter's soul like a white-hot cinder. For Peter had failed. Ministry was confusing. He had done his all and his all was not enough.

I once heard a prominent minister in a megachurch say, 'As I look back at my ministry, I realize that most of it has been conducted in the flesh.' Peter must have felt like that. So I don't beat up on Peter anymore when he says, 'I am going fishing.'

Peter needed time to reflect. He needed time to put all of the pieces together. He was asking the question my friend was asking perhaps. We have a resurrected Savior. And He is calling us to go out and minister. I thought I was doing that. Now I am seeing myself for what I am. I am not sure anymore.

Reflection, as we know, is the beginning of renewal. We all need times of rest and renewal. But maybe you need more. Maybe you are asking, 'Lord, what are You doing in my life, in my ministry? Am I still called? Was I ever called?'

To inquire of God is to draw near to God. Spurgeon spoke of what he called the 'howling Psalms:' those Psalms that begin, 'How long?'

> *My soul also is greatly troubled. But you, O LORD... how long? (Ps. 6:3)*

> *How long, O LORD? Will you forget me forever? How long will You hide Your face from me? (Ps. 13:1)*

> *How long must I take counsel in my soul and have sorrow in my heart all the day? How long shall my enemy be exalted over me? (Ps. 13:2)*

> *How long, O LORD? Will You hide Yourself forever? How long will Your wrath burn like fire? (Ps. 89:46)*

'How long' is the cry of the heart of the minister of Christ who has seen the promises of the Lord meet the pain of living. It is the cry of the soul of the chaplain who authentically brings his burdens to the Lord when all of the ministry tricks he has learned from evangelical magazines and hot best-seller books fall beneath the unforgiving reality of life. And so you cry 'how long?' And you go fishing.

But to read on in the text is to be encouraged that fishing can lead to a catch like never before. And reflection on where you have been and where you are going as a minister of the Gospel can also be the starting point for a new catch—a new commitment to the calling you heard so long ago. In this case, I would ask you, 'Are you just pressing on to the next assignment? Or would you dare join Peter, admit that ministry is really more than you can handle alone, and get in the boat, and reflect?'

So, reflection is the genesis for a renewal of our commitment to our calling. The second word is what follows when we are in the boat of reflection.

RECOGNITION

The scene is amazing. Whether you find Peter to be introspective and reflective, given all that he has seen and all that he knows himself to be, or, in fact, you just see him as a washed up preacher, sort of like a crooked televangelist in the floating cell of his own making. (I cannot see this in Peter unless I see it in my own life.) The thing that happens next is nothing short of spectacular.

Jesus said to them, 'Children, do you have any fish?' They answered Him, 'No'. (John 21:5)

This is where Peter was. No ministry. No fish. No conversions, but also no satisfaction coming out of time in the boat. He was just fishing. But there were no fish.

> *He said to them, 'Cast the net on the right side of the boat, and you will find some'. (John 21:6)*

So they followed the instruction of the bold stranger on the shore. And they cast their nets, like they had done so often before. And there was a catch that they couldn't haul in. I once had a 25-pound catfish on a trotline in South Louisiana. I know how it is! I had to beat that thing in the head with a hammer to kill him to get him in the boat! But they could not get the fish in the boat. And here is the thing: the sea, the boat, the fishing, the lack of fish, the voice, the command, the result…they had experienced this all before. It is in Luke 5:1-11:

> *On one occasion, while the crowd was pressing in on Him to hear the word of God, He was standing by the lake of Gennesaret, and He saw two boats by the lake, but the fishermen had gone out of them and were washing their nets. Getting into one of the boats, which was Simon's, He asked him to put out a little from the land. And He sat down and taught the people from the boat. And when He had finished speaking, He said to Simon, 'Put out into the deep and let down your nets for a catch.' And Simon answered, 'Master, we toiled all night and took nothing! But at Your word I will let down the nets.' And when they had done this, they enclosed a large number of fish, and their nets were breaking. They signaled to their partners in the other boat to come and help them. And they came and filled both the boats, so that they began to sink.*

John recognized it. Then Peter. And Peter dived in. He paused to put on his outer garment. There are many interpretations of this, but all I know is that we do weird things when we come into contact with the One we have been dreaming of, thinking of, and when the guilt or confusion or loss of understanding in sacred reflection is met with the voice of Jesus. You grab your stole again. You grab your old torn pastoral robe. You dress up a bit. You are about to meet Jesus. And so Peter swims for it.

I am here to say, 'Listen as you reflect.' For the one who goes fishing for answers with the Lord will finally hear His voice. You may hear it tonight in this message. Or you may hear it alone with your wife and children on a beautiful mountainous pathway. Or you may hear the voice of your Beloved amidst the ordered chaos of an aircraft carrier, or in the cave of Kandahar. But when you hear, you recognize Him. You recognize His voice.

Maybe you heard the voice of Jesus that called you as a young boy, like Douglas Kelly, one of our professors at RTS Charlotte, who testifies that he heard the voice of Jesus deep in his soul as a five-year-old boy, calling him to give his life to Him as a preacher. Maybe you heard the voice of Jesus when you sat on the lap of your grandmother and she read a Bible story from one of those little books you see in the dentist's office. You heard His voice from His Word calling you to turn to Him. Or maybe, you heard that voice, as I did, as I came in contact with His grace as a young man, and knew that all other pursuits, all other ambitions, were as nothing before the ambition to preach the unsearchable riches of His grace that I had once run from.

But you recognize. And to reflect is to be in a position to recognize. But that leads to a third sacred movement in this renewal of your commitment to the call on your life.

REASSESSMENT

All of us in the military are used to 'After Action Reports.' And this is one big AAR for Peter. The resurrected Christ waits for the right time. After breakfast on the shore, Jesus spoke to Peter. I imagine that Peter knew this was coming. Jesus knew it had to come.

> *Simon, son of John, do you love Me more than these? (John 21:15).*

He did not call him Peter. He called him by his given name, Simon. He had to get back to the beginning. He had to strip away everything. And Jesus dealt with Peter's love of Him. But when Jesus adds 'more than these' He strikes at the heart of Peter's problem. Peter's love was always in competition with others. His relationship with Jesus was, seemingly, as displayed in the New Testament, a matter of performance. It was all about what Peter could do for Jesus. And it was always in the context of 'Others will deny You, but I will never.'

And now this place of pain, where best intentions, made in the flesh, met with worst consequences, played out in time, had to be addressed. Three times Jesus asks Peter 'Simon, son of John, do you love Me?' Peter's love was confirmed. But Peter knew now that his love was a love that responded to the initiation of the love of Jesus. We serve Christ because He loves us. He chose Abraham. He chose Peter. He chooses us. And this is not because of our prowess in the pulpit or our gifts or even our willingness to follow Him. He chooses us out of His love. And our love for Him must in return be the staring point for our ministry. Peter needed to know that. I do too.

Three times Jesus told him to feed or tend His sheep. Peter was called. That was settled. But the reassessment was that the sheep belonged to Jesus not Peter. And the ministry was Jesus' not Peter's. And in fact, Peter's very life and ministry were one. He was to feed the sheep of Jesus out of the overflow of love that He knew from Christ. In the end, his life and ministry were in the hands of others.

But here is the reassessment for all of us. We must minister out of our personal experience of His love, not our strength. Or we could say, in ministry, 'Love Alone is Credible.' This was, of course, the Roman Catholic theologian, Hans Urs von Balthasar's, apologetic (Ignatius Press, 2004). And despite exceptions taken with other significant parts of von Balthasar's theology, I cannot help but say 'Amen' to this part. For as Peter had to learn that Christian ministry begins with an experience of mind and heart in love with Jesus, with a sacred encounter with this most beautiful, loving, forgiving resurrected Savior, so do I. Do you?

When you know that love again in your life you have renewed a commitment to ministry in which His passion flows through you. You say like Paul:

I thank Him who has given me strength, Christ Jesus our Lord, because He judged me faithful, appointing me to His service, though formerly I was a blasphemer, persecutor, and insolent opponent. But I received mercy because I had acted ignorantly in unbelief, and the grace of our Lord overflowed for me with the faith and love that are in Christ Jesus. The saying is trustworthy and deserving of full acceptance, that Christ Jesus came into the world to save sinners, of whom I am the foremost. But I received mercy for this reason, that in me, as the foremost, Jesus Christ might display His perfect patience as an example to those who were to believe in Him for eternal life. (1 Tim. 1:12-16, ESV)

And like Paul, your life, overflowing with His love, breaks out into spontaneous doxology:

To the King of ages, immortal, invisible, the only God, be honor and glory forever and ever. Amen. (1 Tim. 1:17, ESV)

When your vocation becomes doxology, your renewal is complete.

But I have one final word to describe what I see in this text to describe the process of renewing your commitment to Christ's calling on your life.

RE-ENTRY

For immediately after this ethereal experience, this hopeful renewal and restoration of Simon to the Gospel ministry, after reflection and recognition and reassessment, we see glimpses of Peter, the old Peter, once again:

Peter turned and saw the disciple whom Jesus loved following them, the one who had been reclining at table close to Him and had said, 'Lord, who is it that is going to betray You?' When Peter saw Him, he said to Jesus, 'Lord, what about this man?' (John 21:20–21)

Peter had been told that ministry would lead him to death. I don't know about you, but I might have said the same thing, 'What about him?' In Bonheoffer's *The Cost of Discipleship*, his assessment of the call to follow Jesus is always true:

> *When Christ calls a man, He bids him come and die. It may be a death like that of the first disciples who had to leave home and work to follow Him, or it may be a death like Luther's, who had to leave the monastery and go out into the world. But it is the same death every time—death in Jesus Christ, the death of the old man at his call.*

And Peter was renewed, but his renewal brought him on a pathway of growth in that renewal. There would be lapses into the old ways, and face-to-face admonitions by Paul. There would be revelations about the Gospel and the Gentiles. But in the end there would be the man of God, the fatherly pastor, writing to the 'elect exiles' these words from his letter from 'a Birmingham prison':

> *…this is the true grace of God. Stand firm in it (1 Pet. 5:12).*

CONCLUSION

What is at stake? Your family. Your ministry. Your own sanctification. Your example to your children, and to the children of God who look to us. But the reflection of our calling, recognition of His voice, reassessment of our love, and re-entry into the ups and downs of His calling on our life always lead to His passion being dispersed to others. He could have done it through angels. He could have done it through a single cosmic fiat that brought about a new heavens and a new earth. 'But when He ascended on high…He gave gifts to men' (Eph. 4:8). And He gave some to be 'pastors and teachers to equip the saints for the work of ministry' (Eph. 4:11b-12a).

One of those pastors, a giant man of 6'8", the Episcopal rector of Trinity Church, Philadelphia, was never married, except to his calling. It is remembered by some of his people that he kept toys in his study in order to connect with the children of his church, the only children that he claimed as his own. But ministry can be draining. As a single man, with a large parish, with the mundane burdens of Sunday after Sunday bearing down on his large frame and his larger heart, this man must have said, 'I am going fishing.' And he went to Bethlehem. And in 1865 as he worshipped on Christmas Eve at the site where Jesus was born, he obviously came to hear a voice on the shore, if not in the crib. It was a voice that led to a hymn that we sing each Christmas, a hymn that all of you have sung. And the final stanza of Bishop Phillip Brooks' carol has special meaning when we think of our callings before Christ:

> *O Holy Child of Bethlehem, descend to us, we pray.*
> *Cast out our sin, and enter in, be born in us today.*
> *We hear the Christmas angels, the great glad tidings tell.*
> *Oh come to us, abide with us, our Lord Emmanuel!*

Oh, may we too hear that call now. The simple call that Jesus gave to Peter in this passage; the beautiful call that you heard so long ago; the call that He still gives to all who will dive in and swim to Him this day:

You follow Me. (John 21:22)

Oh, Christ Jesus, who called Peter, and who reawakened him to see that our ministries must flow from receiving

Your love, and loving others out of that love, descend to us, we pray. And renew our commitment to Your call. Reshape us so that Your passion for Your ministry of redemption of men and women and boys and girls, of the nations of the earth, will flow through us. We pray this for Your glory and for our families, our churches, our troops, our nation, our generation, and our eternal good. In Jesus' name. Amen.

16

Seminary: A Ministry of Preparation[1]

Nothing can be rightly known if God be not known; nor is any study well managed, nor to any great purpose, where God is not studied. We know little of the creature till we know it as it stands in its order and respects to God; single letters and syllables uncomposed are nonsense. He who overlooks the Alpha and Omega and does not see the beginning and end, and Him in all, who is the all of all, sees nothing at all.—Richard Baxter[2]

Recently I participated in the ordination of a young man to the Gospel ministry, to pastor a congregation in a small town in South Carolina. It was an awe-inspiring moment. And beneath the prayers and petitions, with the laying on of hands, I watched his wife, smiling with tears, holding their babies and looking up to heaven. You see, their

---

1   The following chapter was written as a convocation at RTS.

2   Elliot Ritzema and Elizabeth Vince, eds., *300 Quotations for Preachers from the Puritans*, Pastorum Series (Bellingham, Washington: Lexham Press, 2013).

dreams were coming true. Hard work and commitment to
follow a Savior had now led to this worship service.

And yet three years ago he sat where you sit today:
excited; perhaps with some slight, good anxiety; wondering
about the new start that will lead not to an end, but
to the beginning of a ministry. This is your ministry of
preparation for the journey of a lifetime, of following the
Lord all of the days of your lives, as pastors, missionaries,
teachers, counselors, or other servants of God.

As you begin at seminary, let me draw your attention
to the Scriptures for some thoughts on the blessings of
seminary. I turn to David's Psalm 25, several selected
verses:

> To you, O LORD, I lift up my soul.
> Make me to know your ways, O LORD; teach me your paths.
> Lead me in your truth and teach me, for you are the God of
> my salvation; for you I wait all the day long.
> Remember your mercy, O LORD, and your steadfast love, for
> they have been from of old.
> Remember not the sins of my youth or my transgressions;
> According to your steadfast love remember me, for the sake of
> your goodness, O LORD!
> Good and upright is the LORD;
> Therefore he instructs sinners in the way.
> He leads the humble in what is right, and teaches the humble
> his way.
> All the paths of the LORD are steadfast love and faithfulness,
> For those who keep his covenant and his testimonies.
> For your name's sake, O LORD, pardon my guilt, for it is great.
> Who is the man who fears the LORD?
> Him will he instruct in the way that he should choose.

His soul shall abide in well being, and his offspring shall
inherit the land.
The friendship of the Lord is for those who fear him,
And he makes known to them his covenant
(Ps. 25:1, 4-14, esv)

This Psalm of David focuses on a plea that God would teach the Psalmist the ways of God. There is no higher pursuit than the pursuit of the thoughts and ways of God. We may pursue the ways of God in nature, but His ways can never be apprehended and applied to our lives and families and our culture outside of pursuing God in His Word. For those who are called to be ministers of the Gospel, to go to the ends of the earth as missionaries, to teach others in institutions, or to serve in the work of telling others about God and His ways, one must first be a learner. The disciples sat under the teaching of Jesus before they were sent. St. Paul was sent into the desert for three years and there, we learn in later texts, this tremendous teacher to the Gentiles was taught by God Himself. All ministry begins with a call and then moves directly to the ministry of preparation.

Seminary literally means *'a seedbed.'* This is a *'seedbed'* of pastors and other servants of the Lord. You have come to learn. You are like David crying, 'To You, O Lord, I lift up my soul' for in coming here to this place, you have shown your submission to God in learning. You are a true disciple: one who sits at the feet of the Master. Our pastors here, who serve as teachers of the Word, are but ambassadors of Christ. And through the ordination and authorization of the Church, they are servants to you in the ministry of answering your plea to know more of God. As you cry with David, 'Lead me in Your path and teach me,' we are here to respond, in Christ's name, humbly, prayerfully, dependently, but intentionally and to answer that plea. We answer, in every class and in every thing we do, by giving you the Word of God. We are committed to the inerrant and infallible Word of the Living God as the only way you can have what you need to fulfill the ministry to which God has or will call you.

The context for all of this growth that David desires is summed up in a phrase that is repeated in verses 6, 7 and 10: the steadfast love of God. This phrase is interpreting one Hebrew word: *hesed*. This is the covenant love of God that never ends. It is the love that is personified in Jesus Christ. Jesus said that to know Him is to know life. Jesus said that to know the truth is to be set free. David wants knowledge of God and His grace, he wants to know the freedom—may we say the blessing—that comes from knowing God and His ways in the context of His grace. Your time in seminary is a time to follow like David, in the context of the covenant of grace, to pursue truth and be free. Therefore there are unique blessings to being in seminary and to be pursuing the ways of God.

TO PURSUE THE WAYS OF GOD IN SEMINARY IS TO KNOW A BLESSING FOR YOURSELF

We mark that David cried for God to 'make me know' and to 'teach me.' This is very personal. David desires the teaching of God in his own life.

One thing I want to say to you is that 'your vocation has now become your sanctification.' I will say that to you in the pastoral theology class, but I want to say it to you on this first day in seminary.

Seminary, as it is shaped and formed on the ordinary means of grace in the Bible, will bring about growth in you. You should, as Francis Schaeffer put it, leave loving God more at the conclusion of your years in seminary than at the beginning.

As I remember my time in seminary, there were many nights when I used to go home, after long classes through the day and evening, with absolutely jaw-dropping awe of the God I thought I knew. But as I studied more and more of Him in His Word, led by capable pastor-teachers, in an intensive time of study that you will likely never repeat, I found that I did not know Him like I could. I was being led in His truth. I was beginning to know His ways.

TO PURSUE THE WAYS OF GOD IS TO KNOW A BLESSING FOR OTHERS

We read in verse 13 that the one who fears the Lord will indeed be instructed by God. The result will be that he will not only be blessed (abide in well-being) but 'his offspring shall inherit the land.'

My beloved, as I welcome you to seminary I know that what you are about to embark upon, if you apply yourself to the teaching of the Lord, will be blessed of God to your posterity. Your families will be blessed.

How well I recall going home at night and telling my wife, who was waiting for me with excitement to hear all that I had learned, about this glorious God of grace! My wife was thus blessed by God. Through seminary and my time of pursuing God, however faithful I might have been, it was God's blessing that transformed my home into a seminary. I have been able to teach my children the Word of God, to instruct them in the ways of God that I learned from my time of sitting under godly pastor-teachers in that intensive time of learning called seminary. The offspring of David includes Gentiles as well as the household of Jacob. And so too will your offspring include those who hear you preach in your pulpit, whether that pulpit is in a small local congregation in South Carolina, or a hidden place in a mountain in China, or in a classroom in a university, or as an itinerant evangelist.

My prayer is that you will commit in your heart to pursue the ways of God in order to bless the world with the knowledge of Jesus Christ. I pray that you will not be a container, holding the Gospel to yourself, but a channel through which the knowledge of God flows to the lost, to the needy, to the entire earth. May God bring revival through this class this morning!

FINALLY, TO PURSUE THE WAYS OF GOD IS TO BRING BLESSING TO GOD HIMSELF

King David says in Psalm 25:

To you, O LORD, I lift up my soul,
You are the God of my salvation,
Good and upright is the LORD,
For your name's sake, O LORD.

Throughout the psalm he magnifies the God of the covenant of grace, the *hesed* love of God.

In conclusion, to pursue the ways of God:

1. is to bring honor and glory to God. And this is what the Catechism means when it says, 'The chief end of man is to glorify God and to enjoy Him forever';
2. is to, of course, end up at a manger in the life of Jesus, in His baptism with the anointing of the Holy Spirit, and the testimony of the Triune God that this man of Galilee is in fact Almighty God, the God of the Covenant, the God of steadfast love;
3. will lead you to His passion, to the cross, to the recognition of your sins, to your need for a life lived in righteousness on your behalf before this holy God;
4. will lead you to an empty tomb, and to an open sky with a Savior ascending to His coronation on high. Your pursuit will lead you to the Spirit's sending you out in power to the ends of the earth.

In the end to pursue the ways of God will lead you to knowing Him, loving Him, and glorifying Him in heaven.

That is what the blessing of the pursuit of God will bring. *That* is what I pray seminary will be for you—the beginning of a journey of blessing for yourself, for others, and for God Himself.

Appendix 1
The Ministry of a Seminarian

The worth and excellency of a soul is to be measured by the object of its love: he who loves mean and sordid things does thereby become base and vile. But a noble and well-placed affection does advance and improve the spirit unto a conformity with the perfections which it loves.—Henry Scougal[1]

In the springtime the golden Welsh daffodils gather in glorious brigades—brave, young, mythical sentinels appearing out of the fertile earth, guarding a new countryside painted with a Creator's palette of happy color. Spring lambs are born; in the far pasture a wet Jersey calf hides in the tall, green Rye as its little, light-brown mother licks away the winter womb's wrapping; and sweet little downy chicks run around the hen-house like tiny lemon drops with twigs for legs, chirping a cheerful, new song

---

1   Elliot Ritzema and Elizabeth Vince, eds., *300 Quotations for Preachers from the Puritans*, Pastorum Series (Bellingham, Washington: Lexham Press, 2013).

never heard, yet forever sung: and these things were mine as a child on a truck crop farm in Louisiana. They are, gratefully, mine—ours, now. But that which is being born before me is no longer one of the Lord's little creatures of the field. No, now I see new pastors being born. These dear pastoral foals, wet with the birthing time of systematic theology, classes in Greek grammar and Hebrew exegesis, apologetics and church history, are now springing forth into a new world, with long-legged, wobbly dreams that are often the very thing that trips them up and makes them tumble back to earth, at least for a bit. They are young—newly born, I say—and so they quickly get up and kick up their heels and try to prance like the stallion. Only those watching can laugh the laugh of joy, never mockery, mind you—forbid it to ever be—for we once ran, we once pranced, and we, too, were young pastors in the springtime of ministry. This is the springtime for new pastors. And the Lord saw it. And it was good.

On occasion, I am granted the great honor of being invited to preach the installation or give a charge to these new pastors, fresh from their ordination exams. Sometimes I can't, as in a recent invitation which conflicted with earlier ministry commitments. Yet I seek to write as many of these young pastors as I can. For in them, I see something beautiful—a future of the Church of Jesus Christ which I would not otherwise see. These days I am seeing so much good in these newborn shepherd-lambs. These days I am praising God for a good crop of new springtime pastors who will shepherd the flock better than I did.

Here is a letter I wrote recently. I use it as a prayer for all of you congregations with new pastors and all of you new pastors and all of you pastors who will embrace the spring of this year as the new season of your own ministry, no matter how long it has been since you pranced:

My Dear Fellow Pastor and Sister in Christ and Little Children,

Greetings and congratulations to you in the name of our Lord and Savior Jesus Christ! My friend, I remember, so vividly, being in my study at First Presbyterian Church, Chattanooga, and speaking of the things of God and of the pastorate and of the stirring of the Lord in your life. I remember talking about how seminary would be a blessing to you. I saw your zeal and desire to grow deeper in the word of God and the obvious call of Christ upon your life as a pastor. I knew that a good 'School of the Prophets' would be just the thing to help you prepare for a life of ministry. Now, to see those cherished moments of yesterday to be blessed of God today, and to come to fruition at this time, with your ordination and installation as a new pastor, must be a source of deep satisfaction to you and causes all of us to strengthen our trust in the God who truly completes what He starts (Phil. 1:6).

I'm so sorry that I was unable to attend the service and accept your preaching invitation. Please know that I remain deeply humbled and honored by that sweet invitation. I am certain that the commitments to previous appointments, as worthy as they are, will rob me of a special occasion I would have had with you. Oh how sweet those times are! Yet my prayers are unhindered: I trust and pray the Lord anoints you for ministry so that many souls are claimed for Christ, many lives are transformed, and your hope and your glory and your joy will be those souls—and generations that follow them—safe in the arms of Jesus Christ when He comes again (1 Thess. 2:19-20).

I pray blessings down upon your beloved wife and your dear children. I ask that the leadership of the church, and all the saints, will be happily united in their new pastor and your biblical vision and mission for the Kingdom of God, beginning in your community and unto the ends of the earth. My son in the faith, preach and pray, 'Do the work of an evangelist,' counsel wisely, and serve your congregation out of the fullness of the Holy Spirit in your daily life of prayer. May the pastor of that congregation truly be an 'Enoch' who walks with God. Oh, that your entire life and ministry would overflow from time with Jesus and Jesus alone! Watch out for peddlers who would steer under-shepherds of Christ away from the ordinary means of grace in feeding His lambs. Word, Sacrament, and Prayer call, convert, sustain, and will get your flock home to the Good Shepherd His way.

Be a shepherd, not a CEO.

May your home life, my beloved sister in Christ, be a wellspring of warm and holy hospitality to those who need to know Jesus Christ through you. May your children come to love the Church as they grow in the grace and admonition of the Lord with their father as their pastor. Help him to make your home a 'little church' for your family as much as you desire your church to be a 'little family' for others.

My own family sends their love and greetings to you all. I trust you will give my warm greetings to your new congregation and know that we are proud, in Christ, of you, excited about your ministry, optimistic about the work of Christ in you, and trust that I will always be,

Your Very Thankful Old (former!) Pastor, Your Servant, and Your Colleague in the Gospel of God's Grace,

M.A.M.

Appendix 2
A Hymn for God's Calling of Ministers

I first composed this hymn for Knox Theological Seminary. It has since been recorded and sung on an album, with Michael Card.[1] Yet, I think I prefer it myself sung by a congregation. It was intended for a setting for an ordination, a graduation, a convocation, but is humbly offered now just for meditation and prayer.

GOD IS CALLING FAITHFUL MEN[2]

God is calling faithful men,
Shepherds for His flock to tend;
His the vision, He ordains,
He supplies and He sustains;

---

1 Michael Anthony Milton and Michael Card, 'God Is Calling Faithful Men', Michael Milton with Michael Card, recorded October 5, 2010, Michael Milton, 2010, CD.

2 The hymn may be sung to the tune DIX 7.7.7.7.7.7 (the traditional tune to 'For the Beauty of the Earth') by Conrad Kocher (1838).

CALLED?

God is calling faithful men,
Shepherds for His flock to tend.

Grounded in His Word, their light,
Out they go into the night;
Seeking lambs who've gone astray,
Leading them back to the Way;
God is calling faithful men,
Shepherds for His flock to tend.

Let not many teachers be,
Greater judgments will they see,
But, as they do heed God's call,
Christ becomes their all in all;
God is calling faithful men,
Shepherds for His flock to tend.

Men led by a nail-pierced hand,
Let them pastor in our land,
Feeding us with tender care,
Word and Sacrament and Prayer;
God is calling faithful men,
Shepherds for His flock to tend.

Bibliography

This whole visible world is like a book written by the finger of God—that is, created by divine power; and individual creatures are figures ... established by the divine will to show forth the wisdom of the invisible things of God.—De Tribus Diebus[1]

This bibliography represents an attempt to provide resources that will help the reader do a self-study of the issues related to work, location, and a biblical and theological reflection on the gospel ministry and the work of ordination. I have at times referred to books that deal with pastoral ministry, and other works that deal with the Christian life and work, for instance, only because they contain components of the larger concern that I had in mind. Overall, however, I believe that the inquirer can find quite a good opportunity for self-study and reflection

---

1   David L. Jeffrey, *A Dictionary of Biblical Tradition in English Literature* (Grand Rapids, Michigan: W.B. Eerdmans, 1992).

from these sources. This list is, however, not exhaustive and I am certain that I have left off some fine volumes.

Ascol, Thomas K. *Dear Timothy: Letters on Pastoral Ministry*. Cape Coral, FL: Founders Press, 2004.

Badcock, Gary D. *The Way of Life: A Theology of Christian Vocation*. Grand Rapids, MI: W.B. Eerdmans, 1998.

Balthasar, Hans Urs Von. *The Christian State of Life*. San Francisco: Ignatius Press, 1983.

Baxter, Richard, and Thomas Rutherford. *The Reformed Pastor: Shewing the Nature of the Pastoral Work*. New York: J.C. Totten, 1821.

Beecher, Luther F. *On the Choice of a Profession. An Address Delivered before the Theological Society of Union College. On Sabbath Evening, July 20, 1851*. Albany: Weed, Parsons, 1851.

Benson, R. *The Echo Within: Finding Your True Calling*. Colorado Springs, CO: WaterBrook Press, 2009.

Bridges, Charles. *The Christian Ministry, with an Inquiry into the Causes of Its Inefficiency*. London: Banner of Truth Trust, 1967.

Chapell, Bryan. *Christ-centered Preaching: Redeeming the Expository Sermon*. Grand Rapids, MI: Baker Books, 1994.

Clowney, Edmund P. *Called to the Ministry*. Phillipsburg, NJ: Presbyterian and Reformed Pub., 1964.

Fichter, Joseph Henry. *Religion as an Occupation; a Study in the Sociology of Professions*. Notre Dame, Ind: University of Notre Dame Press, 1961.

Guinness, Os. *The Call: Finding and Fulfilling the Central Purpose of Your Life*. Nashville, TN: Thomas Nelson Inc., 1998.

Hendrix, John. *Finding Your Place in Ministry*. Nashville, TN: Southern Baptist Convention Pr., 1988.

Hood, Edwin Paxton. *Lamps, Pitchers, and Trumpets: Lectures Delivered to Students for the Ministry on the Vocation of the Preacher*. London: Jackson, Walford, and Hodder, 1867.

Keller, Timothy J., and Katherine Leary Alsdorf. *Every Good Endeavor: Connecting Your Work to God's Work*. London: Hodder & Stoughton, 2012.

Kohler, Robert F. *The Christian as Minister: An Inquiry into Servant Ministry in the United Methodist Church*. Nashville: General Board of Higher Education and Ministry, United Methodist Church, 1985.

Kuhrt, Gordon W. *An Introduction to Christian Ministry: Following Your Vocation in the Church of England*. London: Church House, 2000.

LaReau, Renée M. *Getting a Life: How to Find Your True Vocation*. Maryknoll, NY: Orbis Books, 2003.

MacGlinchey, Joseph F. *The Workers Are Few: Reflections upon Vocation to the Foreign Missions*. Boston, Mass: Society for the Propagation of the Faith, 1912.

Martini, Carlo Maria. *Drawn to the Lord: Six Stories of Vocation: Maximilian Kolbe, Thérèse of the Child Jesus, Charles De Foucauld, Simone Weil, Giorgio La Pira, Robert and Christine*. Dublin: Veritas, 1987.

Milton, Michael A. *Leaving a Career to Follow a Call: A Vocational Guide to the Ordained Ministry*. Eugene, OR: Wipf and Stock Publishers, 2000.

_____. *The Secret Life of a Pastor and Other Intimate Letters on the Pastoral Ministry*. Scotland: Christian Focus Publications, 2015.

Montgomery, Felix E. *Pursuing God's Call: Choosing a Vocation in Ministry*. Nashville, TN: Convention Press, 1981.

Nelson, Tom. *Work Matters: Connecting Sunday Worship to Monday Work*. Wheaton, IL: Crossway, 2011.

Parnell, Chris W. *'The Pastoral Call': A Guide to Churches and Pastors*. Place of Publication Not Identified: Baptist Union of South Africa, 1978.

Peterson, Eugene H. *Five Smooth Stones for Pastoral Work*. Grand Rapids, MI: W.B. Eerdmans, 1992.

_____. *The Contemplative Pastor: Returning to the Art of Spiritual Direction*. Grand Rapids, MI: Wm. B. Eerdmans Pub., 1993.

_____. *The Pastor: A Memoir*. New York: HarperOne, 2011.

Piper, John. *Don't Waste Your Life*. Wheaton, IL: Crossway Books, 2003.

Preece, Gordon R. *The Viability of the Vocation Tradition in Trinitarian, Credal, and Reformed Perspective: The Threefold Call*. Lewiston, NY: Edwin Mellen Press, 1998.

Proctor, Samuel D., and Gardner C. Taylor. *We Have This Ministry: The Heart of the Pastor's Vocation*. Valley Forge, PA: Judson Press, 1996.

Quayle, William A. *The Dynamite of God*. New York: Methodist Book Concern, 1918.

Rees, Erik. *S.H.A.P.E.: Finding & Fulfilling Your Unique Purpose for Life: Small Group Study Guide*. Singapore: Campus Crusade Asia, 2008.

Richardson, Charles. *This Is Our Calling*. London: SPCK, 2004.

Robertson, George W. *Am I Called? Basics of the Faith*. Phillipsburg, NJ: P&R Publishing, 2013.

Rodenmayer, Robert N. *We Have This Ministry*. New York: Harper, 1959.

Rose, Ben Lacy. *Confirming Your Call in Church, Home, and Vocation*. Richmond: John Knox Press, 1967.

Roth, Bob. *God's Call and Your Vocation: A Look at Christian Calls and Church Occupations*. Nashville, TN: Section of Deacons and Diaconal Ministries, United Methodist General Board of Higher Education Ministry, 1998.

Satgé, John De. *Letters to an Ordinand: A Study in Vocation*. London: S.P.C.K., 1976.

Schnase, Robert C. *Testing and Reclaiming Your Call to Ministry*. Nashville: Abingdon Press, 1991.

Schuurman, Douglas James. *Vocation: Discerning Our Callings in Life*. Grand Rapids, MI: W.B. Eerdmans Pub., 2004.

Sherman, Amy L. *Kingdom Calling: Vocational Stewardship for the Common Good*. Downers Grove, IL: IVP Books, 2011.

Snow, John H. *The Impossible Vocation: Ministry in the Mean Time*. Cambridge, MA: Cowley Publications, 1988.

Spurgeon, C. H. *Lectures to My Students: Complete & Unabridged*. Grand Rapids, MI: Zondervan Pub. House, 1954.

Turner, H. J. M. *Ordination and Vocation: Yesterday and Today: Current Questions about Ministries in the Light of Theology and History*. Worthing: Churchman Publishing, 1990.

Veith, Gene Edward. *God at Work: Your Christian Vocation in All of Life*. Wheaton, IL: Crossway Books, 2002.

Warfield, Benjamin Breckinridge, and John E. Meeter. *The Religious Life of the Theological Student*. Nutley, NJ: Presbyterian and Reformed Pub.

Willard, Dallas. *Hearing God: Developing a Conversational Relationship with God*. Downers Grove, IL: InterVarsity Press, 1999.

Wright, N. T. *For All God's Worth: True Worship and the Calling of the Church.* Grand Rapids, MI: Eerdmans, 1997.

Also available from Christian Focus Publications...

The
SECRET
LIFE
of a
PASTOR

(and other intimate letters on ministry)

MICHAEL A. MILTON

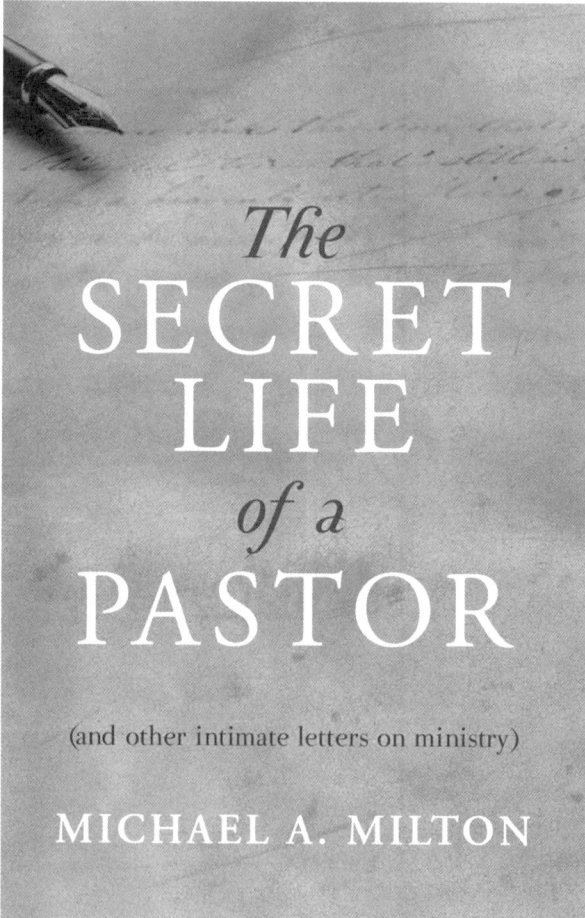

ISBN 978-1-78191-596-7

The Secret Life of a Pastor
(and other intimate letters on ministry)

Michael A. Milton

Living a life of Christian service is tough. Quite rightly we can have big hopes for what can be done and dealing with discouragement and disappointment when these dreams shatter can be a painful experience. Michael Milton has a real heart for those who are beginning that work, this heart comes out in brief, honest, penetrating letters that are gold for a pastor just starting out, and remain tremendously helpful to the rest of us, as we seek to serve Christ in our daily lives.

'… here is a modern version of C. H. Spurgeon's *Lectures To My Students* … they should be read by every pastor, those studying for ministry, and those who care for ministers.'

Paul Kooistra
Former President, Erskine College and Theological Seminary, Due West, South Carolina

'This book is nectar. It is full of rich insights and helpful suggestions that cannot possibly fail to bless the reader and enrich their soul … my advice is: buy it and read it often.'

Tom Holland
Director of Biblical Research, Wales Evangelical School of Theology, Bridgend, Wales

Tim Cooper and Kelvin Gardiner

PASTORING
the PASTOR

Emails of a Journey through Ministry

"Convicting, compelling and ultimately uplifting"
Colin S. Smith

ISBN 978-1-84550-784-8

Pastoring the Pastor
Emails of a Journey through Ministry

Tim Cooper & Kelvin Gardiner

Daniel Donford is a new pastor: excited, filled with bright dreams, anticipating a big future for him and his new church, Broadfield Community Church. However, opposition and obstacles lie just ahead, and both may end his journey into pastoral ministry before it has really begun. But Dan has an Uncle Eldon; if anyone can see Dan through his trials and disasters, Eldon can. The wisdom he offers, via a series of emails, might just be enough to see Dan transformed into the mature, selfless, loving pastor God wants him to be.

'In this earthy and attractive page-turner of a book, we are exposed to the whole fascinating range of Church life and Christian ministry, joys, scandals and all.'

Richard Bewes
OBE, formerly of All Souls Church, Langham Place,
London, England

'Convicting, compelling and ultimately uplifting; this insightful probing of the realities of pastoral ministry will make you smile, lead you to pray, and encourage you to persevere.'

Colin S. Smith
Senior Pastor, The Orchard, Arlington Heights, Illinois and
President, Unlocking the Bible

PT RESOURCES

JONATHAN GRIFFITHS

THE MINISTRY MEDICAL

A health-check from 2 Timothy

DIRECTIONS:

ISBN 978-1-78191-232-4

The Ministry Medical
A health-check from 2 Timothy

Jonathan Griffiths

Paul's instructions and personal model for faithful ministry remain the standard for every generation. They were written to Timothy in the first instance, but they are very much for us pastor-teachers today. The aim of this short book is simply to boil down the instructions Paul gives, and the characteristics of his own ministry that he commends, so that we may see how our own lives and ministries measure up. There are 36 questions from 2 Timothy in this checkup, each forming a chapter. There is also a checklist at the end of the book, going into each question. The book is a challenge, prompt and refresher for any pastor-teacher at any stage of his ministry. It could be read with a group of leaders or elders, taking one or two questions at a time for consideration and prayer.

'… If you're a young or aspiring pastor, then this book really is a must. If you've been in ministry a while then this book may serve as a helpful review. If you're none of these, it will provide a great insight into the burdens, struggles and pressures your pastor will be facing day by day.'

The Evangelical Magazine of Wales

'This is a great book! A very easy read but a challenging one. An ideal read for young pastors just beginning or equally for someone a few years into their ministry.'

Evangelicals Now

Christian Focus Publications

Our mission statement –

STAYING FAITHFUL
In dependence upon God we seek to impact the world through literature faithful to His infallible Word, the Bible. Our aim is to ensure that the Lord Jesus Christ is presented as the only hope to obtain forgiveness of sin, live a useful life and look forward to heaven with Him.

Our books are published in four imprints:

CHRISTIAN
FOCUS

Popular works including biographies, commentaries, basic doctrine and Christian living.

CHRISTIAN
HERITAGE

Books representing some of the best material from the rich heritage of the church.

MENTOR

Books written at a level suitable for Bible College and seminary students, pastors, and other serious readers. The imprint includes commentaries, doctrinal studies, examination of current issues and church history.

CF4•K

Children's books for quality Bible teaching and for all age groups: Sunday school curriculum, puzzle and activity books; personal and family devotional titles, biographies and inspirational stories – because you are never too young to know Jesus!

Christian Focus Publications Ltd,
Geanies House, Fearn, Ross-shire,
IV20 1TW, Scotland, United Kingdom.
www.christianfocus.com